FADED
GLORY

THE CHURCH IN A CULTURAL CRISIS

H. MAURICE LEDNICKY

FADED GLORY

The Church in a cultural crisis

PREFACE

I stepped into the motel parking lot about 7:00 a.m. on a Monday morning in Dallas, Texas. Within minutes thousands of cars whizzed by on the several interstates that junctioned there. As I observed this beehive of humanity racing off to work, suddenly a thought floated through my mind. *What would Jeremiah the prophet say to this generation?* It was quite sobering. I concluded was that his message to this nation would be very similar to what he said to the people who were living in Jerusalem approximately 600 years before the coming of Christ.

This weeping prophet was overwhelmed as he helplessly witnessed the blatant rejection of Jehovah God by His own people. Certainly, he had spiritual insight into the heart of God and spoke prophetically of future events. However, a large portion of his message came straight from *what he saw*—a culture totally unconcerned about pleasing God and doing anything and everything for personal gratification. The sad truth was that the spiritual leaders had fallen prey to the pressure and reminded Jeremiah that he was a country boy who had the wrong message for that intellectually advanced generation. *Peace and prosperity* was the rhetoric they wanted to hear to soothe their collectively corrupt consciences. A loving God would never allow evil to come to His own children. All the while the ominous storm clouds of God's judgment were growing darker and darker.

Has the Church of this generation become enamored with its culture? Or, have we allowed the screaming voices of culture to intimidate us? Both of these possibilities are unscriptural and disconcerting. The *love of this world* and the *fear of man* are strongly condemned in the Word of God.

My plea is that we look at ourselves honestly in light of God's holiness, Christ's sacrifice, and our unworthiness. God's plan is for us to know and experience His glory in all its radiant splendor. In this unique relationship with the Prince of Glory, the Church is to dramatically impact culture, rather than being consumed by it. The Church is to be victorious, distinct from a sinful culture—as *salt and light*—not blended into obscurity and powerlessness.

> *"Worldliness has gone a long way to destroy the church of God. I judge it to be the worst cankerworm that assails us."*
>
> Charles H. Spurgeon

It was my joy to serve as president of an excellent ministerial training college for more than 21 years. As we approached the year 2000, I stood in a morning chapel service and with shameful tears apologized to the students for the moral bankruptcy of our nation that was being handed to them. Where had we failed? I grew up in an America that, while far from perfect, generally honored the Word of God as absolute truth. Obviously, the shift did not occur in one quantum leap. It came ever so gradually. But, in those little things the Church was silent. Today, Bible-believing followers of Jesus are appalled and horrified at the immoral (perhaps amoral) standard that is commonly accepted in our culture. Is the godless agenda of TV, movies, and music simply coincidental? Are the blatant attacks against those who have a strong commitment of faith isolated acts of a few extremists? I don't think so. There can be no doubt that we are in a serious cultural crisis and the Church of Jesus Christ is in the crosshair of the enemy's biggest weapons.

So, how do we go about properly evaluating cultural mores without compromising our faith? Let me suggest a three-way test.

1. <u>Scriptural absolutes</u>

   The Word of God is absolute truth and every action of any culture should consistently align with principles of Scripture. In a pluralistic society, it may seem a far-fetched fantasy to think this could ever be realized. However, our concern at this moment is for the Church. As believers, His Word must be the backdrop against which all of life's decisions are viewed.

2. <u>Spiritual application</u>

   Pollsters repeatedly find amazing similarities in the behavioral patterns of believers and non-believers. Head knowledge alone cannot suffice. *"Faith without works is dead, being alone."* Purported allegiance to Christ is mockery if the child of God cannot be identified from the person who makes no profession of faith. It is as simple as the old adage: practice what you preach.

3. <u>Surrendered actualization</u>

   Conformity to dogmas, creeds, or congregational regulations is merely personal discipline unless it flows from a love relationship with our Lord. (On the other hand, what is too often defined as legalism is nothing more than carnality refusing to be crucified.) Somewhere there must be a Gethsemane experience. Every choice of life must be weighed in the light of eternity, not the pleasures of the moment. The old chorus echoes the message—"the things of this world will grow strangely dim in the light of His glory and grace."

Some would conjecture it is too late. The Church's glory has faded as it has tolerated and accepted more and more of the culture in which it exists. Yes, there are signs that bring distress to the hearts of God-fearing, Christ-honoring, Bible-believing men and women. But there is hope in the One whose very nature is defined by love and mercy.

The Old Testament reveals a God who had multiple opportunities to give up on His people—and ample reason to write them off. Yet, time and again when there was true heart repentance, He forgave and delivered.

The New Testament builds faith that the Church can survive in any culture. Imagine the persecution and atrocities suffered under the likes of Nero or Domitian. Yet, in spite of such a hostile attitude, the Church not only survived but flourished—even in Caesar's household.

The declaration of Christ is still valid. *"I will build My church and the gates of Hades (the powers of the infernal region) shall not overpower it [or become strong to its detriment, or hold out against it]"* (Matthew 16:18, Amplified).

CHAPTER ONE

EVERYONE ELSE IS DOING IT

*"All of the Christians I meet who are amount-
ing to anything for God are Christians who
are very much out of key with their age—very,
very much out of tune with their generation."*

A.W. Tozer

The shift was gradual for Israel. The journey began with obedience as Abraham left Ur of the Chaldees to become the *"father of many nations."* The story unfolds with Isaac and Jacob (Israel). Then Joseph became prime minister in Egypt. However, after Joseph died, a new Pharaoh turned against the Jewish people and forced them into bitter slavery. More than 400 years passed before God raised up Moses to deliver His people from oppression. According to Scripture (Moses' name is mentioned 848 times), *"there arose not a prophet since in Israel like unto Moses, whom the Lord knew face to face"* (Deuteronomy 34:10). In a marvelous display of mercy and love, God miraculously delivered Israel from the cruel bondage they suffered at the hand of the Egyptians.

The Law of Moses was given while the Israelites were in the wilderness. It is detailed, specific and clearly articulated. **This was not to be a democratic society with majority vote determining the rules. God demanded obedience!** Moses warned again and again of the dire consequences for disobedience. He cut them no slack. He understood the depth of human depravity. Before he died, he spoke of the day when they would want to have a king *"like all the nations"* (Deuteronomy 17:14).

Eventually under Joshua's leadership this chosen family/nation crossed the Jordan River and settled in the Promised Land. It would seem this should and could have been the closest thing to Eden since man disobeyed God's instruction. However, the record in the Book of Judges is among the saddest testimonies of man's depravity. It has often been called the Dark Ages of Israel's history. God would raise up a "judge" (there were 15 in all), the people would be delivered from an oppressive enemy, and they would again enjoy a time of peace. But as soon as the judge died, they returned to their wicked ways and violated every aspect of God's law, especially the worship of false gods. The scene is repeated over and over. One would think they would have learned. The mercy of God is impossible to comprehend!

Now this special character named Samuel appears on the stage. In a rare dimension of scriptural detail, his birth, his young life, and his call are outlined. He was a *"prophet"* (1 Samuel 3:20), served as a *"priest"* offering sacrifices (1 Samuel 7:9), and also *"judged"* Israel (1 Samuel 7:15-17). He is the first prophet and the last judge. His personal leadership skills are noteworthy. Samuel could possibly be described as the forerunner of the circuit- riding preacher.

But as he came near the end of his life, the people pleaded for a *"king to judge us like all the nations"* (1 Samuel 8:6). Instead of depending on the Almighty they chose man's way. Samuel was deeply hurt by this, but the Lord assured him, *"They have not rejected you, but they have rejected me, that I should not reign over them. According to all the works which they have done since the day that I brought them up out of Egypt even unto this day, wherewith they have forsaken me, and served other gods, so do they also unto you"* (1 Samuel 8:7,8).

Perhaps one could conclude they were at least partially justified in their request. They were afraid of the future.

Samuel's sons were corrupt and sacrilegious. Yet, the way to resolve spiritual problems is not by employing man's methodologies. God's way are always right and best.

Such a sad commentary of another generation should clearly speak to us. Bible scholars agree that the Jewish people of Old Testament record are a type of the New Testament church. Could we learn something about cultural impact on God's people? Is it necessary to repeat the same bitter lessons? Perhaps there are telltale signs. Let's rummage around to see what will turn up.

• The "little foxes" make a BIG difference

Growing up in a conservative church and home, I have laughingly said that going to church was the only thing we could do—everything else was sin. But somewhere along the way that began to shift. Now we have gone so far to the opposite extreme that one has to search diligently to find anything that is sin.

Often I would have late-nighters with the men in the dorms at the college we served. Invariably they would want to discuss how it was in the old days. These young preachers-in-the-making would sit, dumbfounded by the anti-worldlikeness that had been the norm in those earlier days. In most instances it had not even dawned on them that certain attitudes and activities might damage the quality of spiritual life they were attempting to achieve.

Where did it start? How have we arrived where we are today? Let me conjecture.

1. <u>Economic prosperity</u> became a two-edged sword. Like Israel, we have allowed the blessings of God to become a distraction from utter dependence upon

Him. Surely none of us has an affection for funeral home fans and slatted benches. So, now like *everyone else* we can afford the best money can buy. There is no evil in advancing the cause of Christ in the most excellent manner possible; in fact, the opposite is true. However, the temptation is always lurking in the shadows to turn to human resource and adopt the methodologies normally associated with business corporations. The true Church is never enslaved by its financial status—rich or poor. That sly little fox has now grown up and often eats the choicest grapes.

2. Intellectual substitutes have lulled many into places of spiritual barrenness. It is right and proper, even mandatory, that we *"rightly divide"* the Word of God. No excuses are acceptable for a careless, casual approach to the study of eternal truth as revealed in Scripture. Yet, it must be understood that personal relationship and relevance come by revelation, not merely through well developed intellectual capacities.

> The Word of God presents truth in *principle*;
> the Holy Spirit makes the *personal application*.

Human explanations (apart from God-given wisdom) are woefully inadequate to face the stark realities that often confront us. Humanism, postmodernism and all the other related intellectual pursuits are cancers in the body of Christ. When one is more comfortable confronting the authority of Scripture than accepting it by faith, spiritual disaster is imminent. If pundits are correct, scarcely more than one-half of those who claim to be born-again believers accept the Word of God as the highest authority for faith and practice.

3. <u>Acceptance of contemporary entertainment forms</u> is a giant time consumer and hence a dangerous distraction from the things of God. It hardly seems appropriate (or even possible) to compile an extensive list of contemporary sources of mind-altering entertainment. Perhaps the big three could be identified as music, TV, and movies. Of course, some things are so blatant that many outside the Church reject them and openly speak against them—at times even more forcibly than those who profess to be followers of Christ.

It would be impossible to discuss this without bringing into focus the cultural obsession with sports. It is true the personal and physical disciplines are healthy, both mentally and physically, for the participants. However, it is possible when huge blocks of time (to say nothing of finances) are expended, the spectators can quickly become preoccupied. Few, if any, other aspects of contemporary cultural life have so riveted the attention of both young and old. One can safely conclude that many believers are also serious devotees. It would seem rather naïve to assume there have been no spiritual injuries along the way. I can only imagine what powerful Christians there would be today if an equal amount of time, energy, and discipline was devoted to learning the ways of God and striving for spiritual growth and maturity.

My purpose is not to blast away at everything in sight, but to call us to serious contemplation. These little foxes have made such a huge difference in His church and our personal relationship with the Lord.

> In his seven volume series, **The Decline and Fall of the Roman Empire**, Edward Gibbon lists six reasons for the destruction of the empire:
> 1. The rapid increase in divorce, the undermining of the dignity and sanctity of the home, which is the basis of human society.
> 2. Higher and higher taxes and the spending of the public moneys for free bread and circuses for the populace.
> 3. The mad craze for pleasure, sports becoming every year more exciting and brutal.
> 4. The building of gigantic armaments when the real enemy was within, in the decadence of the people.
> 5. The decay of religion, faith fading into form, losing touch with life and becoming impotent to guide the people.
> 6. The spread of effeminacy—girls looking and acting like men, men looking and acting like girls.

• Excuse my carnality!

"My parents forced all that legalism stuff on me, and I don't plan to do that to my family," the mother firmly told me. She was defending her talented daughter who was playing the piano at the bar in an upscale restaurant.

The apostle Paul met this issue of carnality head on. If you are a baby, you drink milk. When you grow up, you eat meat. He called it *"crucifying the flesh"* and told believers in Ephesus and Colosse to *"put off the old man"* and *"put on the new man"* (Ephesians 4:22-24; Colossians 3:8-14). In both cases the subject is you (understood); in other words, your responsibility is to discipline your life to scriptural obedience. By the grace of God every believer can and should consistently grow into Christlike maturity. To say that we should be more like Christ tomorrow than we are today is more than preacher rhetoric—it is scriptural.

I understand that spiritual warfare never ceases. The carnal nature struggling to survive. Perhaps some of the battles are of our own making. Excusing our carnality and refusing to accept the authority of Scripture in matters of personal behavior is sheer foolishness. It's like sticking your chin out to the devil and daring him to hit it.

> *Legalism is adding another door to the grace of God.*
> *Carnality is refusing to appropriate the grace of God.*

The symbolism of crucifixion was not lost on the New Testament believers. They had witnessed the cruel, shameful death penalty at the hands of the Romans. In the book of Galatians the apostle Paul provides the most eloquent defense against Judaizers (those who insisted on keeping the ceremonial aspects of the Law of Moses.) Yet, in this same book, he frequently addresses the subject of the crucified life. He declares himself to be *"crucified with Christ"* (Galatians 2:20), says those who belong to Christ and are walking in the Spirit *"have crucified the flesh with the affections and lusts"* (Galatians 5:24), and finally proclaims, *"God forbid that I should glory, save in the cross of our Lord Jesus Christ, by whom the world is crucified unto me, and I unto the world"* (Galatians 6:14).

> *Much of the conversation today about "legalism" is nothing more than the flesh seeking an acceptable method for approval and self-justification.*

• No second-hand experiences

I have observed several spiritual fads that have appeared on the front pew of the local church. Some of these extremes have left injured saints strewn across the landscape. Often one wonders how could such good people be caught up with things so obviously beyond scriptural boundaries. My personal conclusion: These were good people so hungry for God's presence and power that they embraced anything that looked like the supernatural. There are no shortcuts. Push-button technology does not work in spiritual matters. The Israelites shouted when the ark came into the camp, but the Philistines captured it anyway. (They quickly decided, however, that they did not want the ark.)

The longer you go without experiencing the supernatural, the easier it becomes to deny its reality.

What parents experience spiritually cannot be included in the estate they pass along to children and grandchildren. It is sobering to hear that there is a revival of spirituality in our nation, but it is often outside the organized church. The Church is God's plan, and it exists not only for His glory but also for mans benefit. Corporate worship (just as the school classroom) is a powerful teacher for the younger generation. In an atmosphere of holy reverence, the Spirit of God will reveal the living Christ.

Now, I risk being considered generational. The high-energy (smoke and lights) entertainment mode of many church-related functions may attract large crowds and be cutting–edge culturally, but a crisis confrontation with the Christ of the Cross demands more than being sustained by one emotional high after another. Reference the feeding of the 5,000 men, beside women and children. When they returned the next day (all the way across the Sea of Galilee) for another free lunch, Jesus began to press the claims of true discipleship. So many of the crowd refused to accept this kind of miracle that Christ even asked His disciples if they were also going to leave Him.

Where is the prayer meeting calling people to wait upon God until hearts are cleansed, lives are changed, and prayers are answered? Where are those who cling to the altar until the light of heaven breaks through upon unsaved family members? No, this is not a call to go back to a past era of history. It is an appeal that we not follow blindly in the path of other generations. Listen to it again. *"And the people served the Lord all the days of Joshua, and all the days of the elders that outlived Joshua, who had seen all the great works of the Lord, that He did for Israel."* But three verses later: *"All that generation were gathered unto their fathers: and there arose another generation after them,* **which knew not the Lord, nor yet the works which He had done for Israel**" (emphasis mine) (Judges 2:7,10.) It is a plea that we learn the true meanings of salvation and discipleship—justification and sanctification.

• Goliath and his brothers

Goliath was a big boy. He was over 9 feet tall and had four brothers of equal size and demeanor. His thundering challenge to the army of Israel sent cold chills down the spines of even the bravest among Israel's warriors. It was to be a fight to death. Only one would come out alive. It likely brings a smile to your face and a "yes!" to your mind when you recall how young David was so angered by Goliath's contempt for the Almighty that he volunteered to accept the challenge (1 Samuel 17). Of course, it was the Lord who won that battle. The point is that David refused to be intimidated by the bellowing threats of a godless pagan.

In a recent article on the editorial page of a large newspaper, a professor of religion at a major university advocatedg the legalization of prostitution. After giving a strong defense that prostitution was nothing more than providing a service (something any employee does), he launches into a tirade against Christian principles: "Now, we can start a discussion concerning the sacredness of the body. I would expect such a discussion to commence; it is only natural for *people who are as exclusive as Christians to jump on some tired, hackneyed, antiquated bandwagon that criticizes fiercely like a thundering chariot of fire destroying all evil in its wake*" (emphasis mine).

Amazingly, those who champion the cause of political correctness and tolerance are often in the same vocal crowd who are bashing Christians. Believers are identified as the intolerant bigots, accused of being the most likely to incite violence at an abortion clinic or against homosexuals. How sad that many pulpits have fallen silent on serious moral issues. How sad that many who profess faith in Christ have been intimidated into hiding on the job or on the university campus. Even sadder still is that some have taken up the cultural agenda in the name of tolerance (a subject in a later chapter).

• Keeping up appearances

During the reign of King Solomon (David's son), he crafted some shields of pure gold. According to 1 Kings 10 there were 500 of these magnificent shields. Two hundred had 15 pounds of gold; 300 were smaller, a mere four pounds of gold. Just pocket change.

When Solomon's son Rehoboam was king in Judah, Shishak, king of Egypt, attacked Jerusalem and ransacked and plundered the palace and the temple. Among things he carried off were the beautiful gold shields. The scriptural record notes: *"Rehoboam made bronze shields as substitutes...and whenever the king went to the Temple of the Lord, the guards would carry them"* (1 Kings 14:25-28).

Perhaps we, like the ancient king, could be guilty of substituting brass for gold. Consider how it could happen.

Activity for Authenticity

Ritual for Reality

Success for Submission

Meditate on these things and allow the Spirit to speak directly into your life. There is no substitute for an intimate relationship with God the Father, God the Son, and God the Holy Spirit.

• Success is the wrong word

<u>Comparisons</u> and <u>competition</u> are deadly when employed by the Church. At ministers meetings the conversation frequently relates to the previous Sunday's attendance. (I often wonder if the person asking is not really wanting to tell.) Size of congregation, seating capacity of the new facility, amount of missions giving are significant only as they are advancing the cause of Christ. Our Lord *"humbled Himself"* to establish the Church and is the indisputable Head of this spiritual body. Surely, we can do no less as members of His bride in preparation for the eternal wedding.

> *Because we want to become great,*
> *He became small.*
> *Because we will not stoop,*
> *He humbled Himself.*
> *Because we want to rule,*
> *He came to serve.*

Submission, rather than success, must be the deepest longing of every believer. At some point in our Christian walk, there must be a Gethsemane. While Christ endured the physical and emotional suffering of the cross after His prayer of submission, *"Father, if thou be willing, remove this cup from me: nevertheless not my will, but thine, be done"* (Luke 22:42), He had already won the victory.

> Jesus said, *"I will build My church."*
> He did not say, "I will build your church,"
> nor did He say, "You will build My church."

• Blessings are for a higher purpose

Research indicates that some believers have two or three home churches and, depending on the mood of the day decide which they will attend on any given Lord's Day. For such people the church exists exclusively for their own personal benefit. But do the blessings of God flow into our lives without concomitant responsibility? I think not. It is the young child who expects a surprise every time he or she visits with grandparents. As the child matures, reciprocal love develops that desires to give rather than always being the recipient.

How refreshing to find someone who has a servant's heart. Expecting nothing in return, willing to do whatever is necessary, never distressed by the lack of commitment in others, he or she simply and quietly goes about serving our Lord and His Church. Great will be the eternal reward of such a saint.

EMBRACING THE TRUTH

1. The Church is a spiritual organism and must not be servant to any aspect of culture that violates scriptural truth.

2. The Word of God, illuminated by the Holy Spirit, provides understanding to discern between man's self-justifying philosophies and God's eternal purposes.

3. Each generation (and individual) must personally experience God's presence and power. Failure to do so sets the stage for gradual rejection of a holy lifestyle.

4. The true Church will never be fully embraced by an unrenegerate culture. As both Scripture and history verify, believers often become the target of vile men who attempt to destroy through intimidation and accusation.

5. **God's mercy is incomprehensible—Christ is building His church at hell's gate—no cultural virus will succeed in corrupting true believers.**

CHAPTER TWO

THE FINE LINE BETWEEN RELEVANCE AND COMPROMISE

"One of our greatest tasks is to demonstrate to the young people of this generation that there is nothing stupid about righteousness."

A.W. Tozer

Jesus broke tradition. In today's language, He thought outside of the box and developed new paradigms. He ate with sinners. He healed on the Sabbath. For this He was scorned bitterly by the Pharisees and other religious leaders of His time. Although they fabricated many accusations, there was never one shred of evidence that He violated the law of God. While Jesus was relevant to the needs of His culture, He did not compromise scriptural principles.

Anyone who takes the Great Commission seriously agrees that <u>methodology</u> is always to be subservient to the <u>message</u>. Conversely, those same committed believers will agree you cannot catch all kinds of fish with the same bait. The Church has a formidable task in presenting the eternal truth of God's Word in a manner that will stimulate interest—both to believers and unbelievers—without diluting the message.

The bottom-line truth is that believers must be sensitive to the guidance of the Holy Spirit if the spiritual harvest is to be gathered. We have often heard that it is possible to win the battle but still lose the war. Stubborn, inflexible believers who insist on doing it the way it has always been done simply to satisfy their own preferences can seriously hinder the evangelization of this generation. Likewise those who follow every new fad for the sake of being contemporary run the risk of either diluting or confusing the message of the gospel.

Perhaps one of the tests that can be applied is observed in the spirit of the individual. While it is possible for a person who is in gross error to have a good attitude, it is more common for such an individual to become a voice for that cause. Often every other aspect of spiritual reality is measured by one's involvement in this new revelation. Spiritual elitism develops. Others are, to say the very least, not as spiritually perceptive. This historically happens during times of a special visitation (renewal) among God's people. In their zeal, those who have been abundantly refreshed may assume that everyone else must respond in the manner they did in order to receive the fullness of God's blessings. Attempts to force others into a particular style or pattern of worship foster a spirit of judgmental disunity. However, the genuine work of the Holy Spirit brings harmony among true believers. Regardless of whether one is pro or con, the Spirit does not produce harsh anger and bitter disputing.

Even believers of long history will not always respond in a spiritually mature manner. Such behavior is surely not our Lord's plan or desire for His church. In this world of constant change, the elders must have the grace to lovingly help the younger (spiritually and chronologically) find scriptural balance. *To categorically reject every new or different style or method is a recipe for disaster. To categorically accept every new or different style or method is equally a recipe for disaster.* As John the Beloved often prayed, *"Little children, love one another."*

> The ability and/or willingness to distinguish between principle and preference presents a challenge to every generation, regardless of age. The older—because they have formulated strong opinions based on a multitude of experiences; the younger—because it is their only experience.

In spite of the challenges in finding that narrow pathway between relevance and compromise, it is possible to do so. Christ did not exclude this generation when He promised to *"build my Church"* at the very gate of hell itself.

Consider a few items of relevance.

THE MUST-DO LIST

- **Communicate in the common language**
  Today it cannot be assumed that nonbelievers have any knowledge of Scripture. Bible stories that almost everyone knew (i.e., Jonah and the whale, Daniel in the lion's den, etc.), several decades ago are stranger than fiction to this generation. Further, since we are no longer an agricultural society, many of today's urban and suburban dwellers have no clue as to the application of the illustrative material of New Testament narratives and parables (i.e., parable of the sower and the seed). Words such as <u>regeneration</u>, <u>justification</u>, <u>born again</u>, <u>sanctification</u>, *holiness* are foreign to many vocabularies today, even among believers. These truths must be explained in a manner that will connect with the contemporary mind.

Allow me to illustrate with a personal experience. I was ministering in West Africa and one night the Spirit directed me to Luke 10 when Jesus was visiting in the home of Mary and Martha, sisters of Lazarus. Martha was quite busy preparing the appropriate meal or refreshments for the guests. But Mary had chosen to sit and listen to the teaching of Christ. Martha solicited the assistance of the Master in rebuking Mary for not being out in the kitchen. Jesus responded, *"My dear Martha, you are so upset over all these details! There is really only one thing worth being concerned about. Mary has discovered it—and I won't take it away from her"* (Luke 10:41,42, NLT).

As I was preaching, it suddenly dawned on me that this audience more fully understood this story than I ever had. First, they were extremely hospitable. Regardless of economic status, each guest in their homes was offered a meal or refreshments. Second, the women normally did not engage themselves in conversation with the men. Here it was so clearly being articulated by Christ himself. As important as your cultural structure is—being hospitable and following the accepted role for women—there is something of greater significance. That night scores of men and women came to know Christ as personal Lord and Savior. They identified with the message.

Personal experience is a powerful tool for communicating the gospel. It is the truth applied to real-life situations. Among theologians this is defined as contextualization and is acceptable as long as it does not overshadow nor alter the sacred message from God.

- ## See conversion as revelational rather than intellectual
  Simon Peter proclaimed, *"Thou art the Christ, the Son of the living God"* (Matthew 16:16). Christ emphatically stated that this knowledge came from divine revelation, not from intellectual pursuit.

  Thomas cried, *"My Lord and my God,"* when he saw the resurrected Christ (John 20:28), ascribing deity to Him. The apostle Paul speaks frequently of the *"mystery"* that was made known to him by revelation. In light of his own relationship with Christ, Paul denounces his intellectual heritage as being worthless in his compelling desire to *"know him in the power of his resurrection, and the fellowship of his sufferings"* (Philippians 3:10).

In a postmodern culture which defiantly declares there are no absolutes, it is literally impossible to intellectually convince a person of the validity of salvation. If the Word of God is not held as a common starting point (*"Faith cometh by hearing and hearing by the Word of God"*), then only the miracle of divine revelation can capture a mind and change a sinful heart.

Having spent a major segment of my ministerial years training men and women for vocational ministry, I am compelled to sound a warning even to the greatest of inquiring minds. Perhaps this is my soap box. Often in the name of scholarship, some new truth is discovered. It seems that most often the end result is revisionism that compromises some basic tenet of faith long held dear by the saints of God. *The principles of the Word of God are illuminated and applied by the Holy Spirit—not by man's intelligence.*

Once again, the Church must intercede for lost men and women. If an intellectual defense of the gospel does not work, how can "smoke and mirrors" break through a deceived and darkened mind? Do you want to be relevant to this generation? Then pray, pray, pray for the spirit of the Evil One to be bound and the Holy Spirit to bring conviction of sin and reveal the propitiatory Savior.

- **Understand spiritual development to be a process**
  Baggage? This generation has wagon loads! Abuse, incest,

abortion, sexual promiscuity, pornography, drugs, alcohol, divorce, dysfunctional families—where does the list end? The results are lingering hurts, anger, mistrust, all producing a distorted picture of a loving, compassionate Heavenly Father.

Deliverance is often instantaneous. Healing takes time.

We understand the growth process in children and grandchildren. Over and over we instruct; at times we find it necessary to discipline and correct. But we surely do not stop loving them or conclude they will never learn. From years of working with young people in their late teens and early twenties, I found that many of them were actually seeking guidelines. If such boundaries were absent during their formative years, it was as though they were floundering for direction and seeking someone who cared enough to lovingly draw the line.

Never give up on the absurd and outwardly testy person. Who knows? He or she may become a great missionary pastor or when that creative energy is focused on the lordship of Christ.

- **Be willing to accept rejection without rejecting**
  I am overwhelmed by Christ's words on the cross, *"Father, forgive them, for they know not what they do."* How could He do this?
  1. His singular reason for being on earth was man's redemption.
  2. He knew He was accomplishing His Father's will.
  3. He saw beyond the present to the eternal.
  4. He loved enough to personally accept the penalty justly deserved by others.

Rejection is painful. Especially is this true when one has tried desperately to be helpful. Of course, every child of God knows experientially that the personal benefits of salvation are beyond description—both in the present and future life. To be rebuffed for offering the only hope for man is often hard to take.

REMEMBER:

1. This is a spiritual battle, not a personal one.
2. It is the lordship of Christ being rejected, not yours.
3. You are instructed to forgive others as *"God for Christ's sake"* has forgiven us.
4. You may be the only spiritual connection in that individual's life.
5. Never discount the grace of God and the work of the Holy Spirit.

- **Authenticate verbal message as an avid practitioner of your faith**

  Jesus was tough on the Pharisees, Sadducees, and scribes who challenged His authority as God's only Son. Few preachers today have the audacity to call others *snakes, fools, hypocrites, blind, extortioners,* and *inwardly unclean.* He warned His followers not to be like them. Why? Because these spiritual leaders made a major production of external rightness, but they miserably failed to practice what they preached.

> *Influence is the by-product of consistency.*

"I didn't think Christians did things like that" is an accusation often hurled by a self-justifying generation. Yet, maybe the truth is that on the sly they have been carefully watching the lives of believers. They want to know, "Is this really real? Will it work for me? What makes this person so different when he has the same kinds of problems I have?" Amazing isn't it—the perception so many have of the genuine and the phony.

Seated on the platform in the daily campus chapel services, I observed it over and over again. A gifted speaker would address the student body. He or she would deliver the message with excellence. It had to be given high marks—hermeneutically, homiletically, and grammatically. Yet those students sat there stone faced. On other occasions, a less polished speaker would be in the pulpit and there was a resoundingly positive response. The difference? I noted one common denominator. The students perceived (correctly or incorrectly) a transparent reality in one and not in the other. Of all the things necessary to influence this generation spiritually, one quality must top of every list: **Be genuine!**

• Stay focused—allow the Spirit to give direction

The Book of Acts is a powerful workbook for the Church in this generation. The record of how the Holy Spirit was at work in the formation and development of the infant New Testament church is incredible. But notice that there is no "Amen" at the conclusion of Acts 28. The Church of the 21st century is still the New Testament church. The work of the Holy Spirit, the miracles, healings, supernatural manifestations, gifts of the Spirit, and divine guidance did not cease with the completion of the canon of Scripture. *"Jesus Christ the same yesterday, and today, and forever"* (Hebrews 13:8).

Can we still believe for the healing of the lame man at the temple gate? (Acts 3:1-8)

Are there deacons like Philip who will go to Samaria to preach the gospel? (Acts 8:5-8)

Is there a Philip who will leave a great revival to go into the desert to meet one man? (Acts 8:26-38)

Is there another Simon Peter who will hear the Spirit's direction to minister to the Gentile centurion Cornelius? (Acts 10:1-48)

Are there still Antioch assemblies that will send forth missionaries? (Acts 13:1-3)

Can we find a Paul who will hear the Macedonian call, *"Come over and help us"*? (Acts 16:9)

Dare we pray with authority for deliverance from demon powers? (Acts 16:16-18)

Are believers still miraculously protected and delivered as the Scriptures indicate?

If we answer that God has not changed—and He surely has not—then by the same power that thrust the Early Church forward, it is excitingly possible to see the strongholds of Satan invaded, broken, and destroyed today.

THE MUST-<u>NOT</u> DO LIST

• Interpret Scripture to accommodate culture

Recently a major church denomination that espouses the Word of God as the highest level of authority for faith and conduct altered its position on a matter that had been in its doctrinal creed since the founding days of the organization. This happened for one of two reasons. The fallout from either is likely to have a negative impact on the spiritual influence of this group in today's moral climate.

1. <u>Change in hermeneutic.</u> That is, their interpretation of Scripture was revised. What at one time was

strongly believed now was given another slant based on a different approach to how certain passages of Scripture are explained. This plays right into the hands of those who look for any excuse to call into question the authority of Scripture. If dedicated believers can declare one thing for many years and then decide it really does not mean exactly what has been taught, how free are those who love to pick-and- choose from God's Word to determine what is or is not relevant to their lives.

2. <u>Accommodation of culture.</u> If, indeed, the doctrinal creed was altered based on anecdotal information specifically unique to contemporary culture, this is even more tragic. Does the Word of God change to fit each generation? Where do we go next? What other portion of that which is held sacred will come under question? **The Church becomes less and less powerful the more it takes on the characteristics of culture.**

Lest one draw an erroneous conclusion, it must be stated that no individual or organization can realistically claim to be the final word on all truth. Certainly, brilliant scholars who love Christ supremely differ at times on various issues of scriptural interpretation. However, altering a long-standing creed for the sake of becoming more relevant is, at least, a dangerous road. Both within and without there will be confusion. If the *"trumpet gives an uncertain sound"* the gospel is not being properly and clearly communicated.

- **Adopt cultural behavioral patterns as a means of evangelism**

<u>What's wrong with this picture?</u> He sat in a dimly lit bar slowly sipping a drink (not Coke or Pepsi) as a scantily clad singer crooned in a sensuous voice. He is telling the

person on the next bar stool how dramatically his life had been changed since he met Christ.

<u>What's wrong with this picture?</u> The young man joins a heavy metal band, has tattoos all over his body, with ears, eyelids, tongue, and other body parts pierced. His purpose is to identify with this generation so he can share his faith in Christ.

<u>What's wrong with this picture?</u> The highly respected businessman adds his signature to a questionable contract. He not only fears for his job, but he does not want to be considered an outsider. By being one of the crowd, he hopes to have more opportunities to invite his friends to receive Jesus Christ.

You don't have to adopt the world's lifestyle to convince them of your love for them.

The words of scripture ring clear. *"Do not be unequally yoked up with unbelievers—do not make mismated alliances with them, or come under a different yoke with them (inconsistent with your faith). For what partnership have right living and right standing with God with iniquity and lawlessness? Or how can light fellowship with darkness? What harmony can there be between Christ and Belial (the devil)? Or what has a believer in common with an unbeliever? So, come out from among (unbelievers), and separate (sever) yourselves from them, says the Lord, and touch not (any) unclean thing..."*
(2 Corinthians 6:14-17 Amplified).

"For to be carnally minded is death: but to be spiritually minded is life and peace" (Romans 6:6).

"Know ye not that the friendship of the world is enmity with God? Whosoever therefore will be a friend of the world is the enemy of God" (James 4:4).

I am convinced that the world is not looking for a better "pigpen". It is because the believer's life is different that those who are mired in sin are attracted. Showing the peace, joy, and fulfillment of life in Christ is the best advertisement you can present. They really don't want you to act like they do and could care less if you look like they do. Show them Jesus. That is sufficient.

EMBRACING THE TRUTH

1. The Great Commission mandates that we share the gospel with everyone, regardless of cultural distinctions that may be distasteful to the believer.

2. Believers must be wise and sensitive, led by the Holy Spirit in ministering to the spiritual needs in their culture.

3. Two great dangers facing true evangelism are <u>compromise of scripture</u> and <u>accommodation of culture</u>.

4. The church of Jesus Christ desperately needs mature saints who are willing to love and nurture younger believers in spiritual growth and development.

CHAPTER THREE

TOLERATING THE INTOLERABLE

"Men never do evil so completely and cheerfullyas when they do it from religious conviction."

Blaise Pascal

Ordaining practicing homosexuals into the ministry? Condoning or keeping silent concerning the sins of abortion or euthanasia? Youth groups attending R-rated movies as a church-sponsored event? Defending those who deny the substitutionary work of Christ on the cross as the only plan for man's redemption? It is little wonder the unchurched have a difficult time with the organized church.

Revival movements of earlier years have progressively, step by step, abandoned God's plan for holy living. In many church circles today anything and everything is deemed acceptable behavior. Even among evangelical and Pentecostal congregations one is often surprised at the high level of tolerance for that which is blatantly sinful and specifically addressed in the Word of God.

"I'm still praying about it, Preacher," he defiantly told me when I pointed out an unscriptural pattern in his life. The truth is, there are some things you do not have to pray about. If God's Word says *"Thou shalt"* then you are wise and obedient to do it. If it says *"Thou shalt not"* the meaning is quite clear—don't. Our culture has tampered with the simplicity of right and wrong. It would be safe to assume that in most congregations there are some who have adopted the cultural mindset. The prevailing attitude is something like this: What is right or wrong for you may or may not be right or wrong for me. Surely we grasp the diversity in personalities and preferences; however, that is not the point of reference here. The fact is many have gone too far in explaining away the clear meaning of Scripture in attempting to justify themselves or not be offensive to the unregenerate culture. Either is unacceptable to a holy God. Hear the admonition of Paul: *"If I preach circumcision...then is the offence of the cross ceased"* (Galatians 5:11).

- ## Tolerance has to be defined scripturally

Tolerance. Now there's a word for this hour. New Testament believers are tagged as *intolerant bigots* when they speak out against gross immorality (abortion, euthanasia, incest, homosexuality, adultery, fornication) that plagues this generation at every level. Amazingly, the Bible is often quoted as the basis for winking as such detestable sin.

From the fiery pens of Old Testament prophets to the unflinching instruction of the early apostles to *"put off the old man,"* one can find no excusing of sin. Thank God for His abundant grace. Without it none of us could have either present or future hope. ***But there is a major distinction between forgiveness of sin and tolerance of sin.*** The words of Christ are clear. *"Neither do I condemn thee: go, and sin no more"* (John 8:11).

Components of biblical tolerance:
1. God's purpose is redemption.
2. God's authority is Christ's substitutionary suffering.
3. God's nature is long-suffering.
4. God's plan is eternal.

The church of Jesus must not be confused nor intimidated by this culture. The declaration of truth from the pulpit and by those whose ministry is to family, friends, and business associates must give a certain sound. Rise up, men and women of God. Be strong in the Lord and in the power of His might. Judgment day is coming, and we must warn this generation, lest their blood be upon our hands.

- ## Biblical holiness is still God's plan for the Church

Some believers find the word *holiness* to be offensive. It plunges like a dagger into the fleshly nature and requires its daily crucifixion. And, that is painful. But, if I am willing to follow in full obedience to Almighty God, that is exactly what must happen.

Did you know? *The words "holiness" and "holy" are used more than 650 times in Scripture* (King James Version).

There is no room for doubt—God requires His own people to live lives of separation from the world.

1. Israel was not to intermarry with pagans. It would be a step toward accepting and worshipping false gods. (When have you last heard a sermon on "not being unequally yoked together with an unbeliever"?) Ultimately they were taken into Babylonian captivity for worshipping idols.

2. Achan took the forbidden money and clothing from Jericho. God judged the whole nation of Israel for his covetous heart with the loss of the battle at the small town of Ai. God required them to avoid those things associated with evil.

3. Samson allowed the sensuous Delilah to turn his heart from righteousness. He not only lost his hair, he lost his eyesight and his freedom as a result of sinful disobedience.

4. David lusted after Bathsheba and it cost a horrible price. More sin followed. He killed Uriah, Bathsheba's husband. Consider the appalling consequences. One of David's sons, Amnon raped his half sister. Another son, Absalom created an insurrection and tried to steal his own father's throne.

5. Ananias and his wife Sapphira lied about the offering they gave to the infant New Testament church. They both died instantly for making such a false claim. God did not need their money, but He did want pure hearts.

> *Holiness is a heart relationship with Almighty God; righteousness is the product of that relationship.*
> *You can be righteous without being holy;*
> *but it is impossible to be holy without being righteous.*

The apostle Peter says it succinctly: *"Therefore, prepare your minds for action; be self-controlled; set your hope fully on the grace to be given you when Jesus Christ is revealed. As obedient children, do not conform to the evil desires you had when you lived in ignorance. But just as he who has called you is holy, so be holy in all you do; for it is written: 'Be holy, because I am holy'"* (1 Peter 1:13-16, NIV). (Also, Leviticus 11:44-45; 19:2; 20:7).

Faithful saints grieve deeply over what is happening in many quarters of the Lord's church today. The syncretistic blending of biblical truth and cultural mores inevitably lowers the bar of righteousness. If Christ is not all in all, then it follows that His rightful headship of the Church will be compromised. We have no right to decide for ourselves what we consider acceptable behavior. His Word, eternal and unchanging, precisely and clearly articulates His expectations of His children. This is not some form of sadistic demagoguery; it is the benevolent hand of a loving Father who knows what is best for His children.

• Spiritual leaders must be spiritual

Jeremiah saw the inconsistencies and wept. *"The prophets prophesy lies, the priests rule by their own authority, and my people love it this way. But what will you do in the end?"* (Jeremiah 5:31, NIV).

How tragic if a man or woman called by God to be His spokesperson develops an elevated view of his/her own worth. After all, God can make it without us.

In many instances there is grave danger in what is usually termed success. Perhaps every child of God has been tempted along the way with the sparkle of earthly treasures that appeal to the fleshly desires: **Position— Prominence—Power—Prosperity**. Keep your natural and spiritual eyes and ears wide open and alert at all times. Satan is extremely subtle.

1. *Proclaim the whole counsel of God*
   The adage, "The pie has to be sliced the same for everyone" applies here. You cannot pick and choose the portions of Scripture that you deem appropriate for your own life or for justifying the wrong deeds of others.
   This may come across as harsh and unbending to some; really it is not. Either the entire Word of God

is inspired, true, and relevant to this generation or none of it is. I choose to believe that God meant what He said and has not changed His mind because it is the 21st century.

2. *Possess spiritual discernment*
Obviously, holiness cannot be legislated. External (behavioral) righteousness may be demanded for a time, but will surely be short lived. The matter of spiritual discernment is no major mystery if one chooses to live by divine precept. Scriptural principles are applied fairly easily for those fully committed to a personal relationship with Christ. How different would our perception of this world be, if we saw it through the eyes of our Lord. We can— if only we will.

YOU CAN'T LEAD FROM THE MIDDLE

• The picture is out of focus

In an indoor camp meeting where I was preaching one of the pastors pointed out a young man to me during the prayer time around the altar. It was apparent this college-age teen was serious with God. But the pastor related to me that the boy's father had offered him an expensive bribe (new car at graduation) not to consider the ministry. The father's comment was, "You are too smart to spend your life in the ministry. You can make money and support others." He inferred that others were not smart enough to make money or the ministry was of lesser importance than having earthly possessions.

1. <u>Redemption is the heart of the gospel</u>
In the Great Commission (Matthew 28:18-20; Mark

16:15) are two major components: Believers are to make converts and train them. In the words of Christ we are to *"make disciples"* (NIV) in the whole world. This command is to not only lead them to the saving knowledge of Christ, but also to guide them into a mature understanding of His Word. A *disciple* is a student—a *disciplined* follower of his teacher.

Much turmoil troubles the Church today as to what is right and wrong. There are so few disciples. Our relationship with Christ must be more than a one-time prayer to secure a promised escape from eternal damnation. That may be the initial reason for coming to Him, but enfolded in His love and grace one soon discovers that the price for redemption was so costly that his/her overwhelming response is to walk in humble obedience.
Lord, help us to know how much You love us and do everything within our power to reciprocate that love as your grateful servants.

Neo-universalism—the insidious teaching that everyone with eventually be eternally saved because God is too good to send anyone to eternal damnation has slithered its way back into the mainstream of Christian thinking today. Unfortunately it plagues the most conservative of communions. Even among students preparing for a redemption ministry, the question often surfaces. How can God punish those who have never heard? The logical conclusion to such unscriptural reasoning is simply not tell the person who has never known—he/she will be better off. But this idea does not square with Romans 1.

How sad that so many of our church dollars are disbursed for our own comfort and convenience rather than to reach the lost. Of himself, Jesus said, *"And I, the Son of Man, have come to seek and save those like him (Zacchaeus) who are lost"* (Luke 19:10, NLT). Any body of believers following the patterns of a self-indulgent, self-gratifying culture will soon veer from the biblical mandate for the Lord's church.

2. <u>Christ MUST have first option in every life</u>
   A Sunday School teacher posed this question to his class of approximately 100 students: "How many in this room have a direct influence on a young person...son, daughter, grandchildren, other family member or friend?" Everyone in the group responded affirmatively. Then he offered a second question. "How many of you have discussed the claims of Christ with that young person within the past twelve months, including the possibility that He may be calling them into full time Christian service?" This time, no one responded in the affirmative.

   Where are we headed, Church of the living Christ? Have we indeed come to *"have a form of godliness, but deny the power thereof"*? Do we prefer to have our conscience appeased with motivational warm fuzzies? What dreams and goals do parents have for their children? Everyone wants the very best for children and grandchildren. That is scripturally proper and right. But, have they been placed on the altar of commitment to God's will? Is the earnest, daily parental prayer that he or she will follow and serve Christ—regardless of where that path may lead or what it may cost in earthly benefits and rewards? As candid as it may sound, the Church of tomorrow is following the example set before them today. Outside of a divine work of grace, it will react negatively to the emptiness of a profession that has little or no reality.

3. <u>Accountability—to the Church?</u>
In 1961 Elton Trueblood wrote these penetrating words in his volume, **The Company of the Committed.**

"One of the surprising facts about the early Church was its fundamental similarity to a military band. This is so hard for us to recognize today because the ordinary successful church of the twentieth century is about as different from an army as anything we can imagine. Instead of being under anything resembling military discipline we pride ourselves on our 'freedom.' We go and come as we like; we serve when we get around to it. Obedience is considered an irrelevant notion, and the theme of 'Onward Christian Soldiers' is so alien to our experience that some churches avoid the hymn entirely.

"Indeed, military language can be found in various parts of the New Testament. It need hardly be said that this language had no reference to killing, but rather to the mood of men and women whose responsibilities were of the same demanding character as those of enlisted persons.

"It cannot be too emphatically pointed out that such 'service' was not remotely similar to what we call a 'service' today, a polite gathering of auditors, sitting in comfortable pews listening to a clergyman and a choir." 1.

Enough said!

• It can't happen to us

The people in the land of Judea never really believed they would be taken captive by the Babylonians. Oh yes, their relatives, the Israelites, had already been overrun by the Assyrians, but that was different. In spite of warning after warning by God's anointed prophets, they just kept right on sinning—until judgment came.

Had you asked the leadership of a host of communions half a century ago if they could envision the day their church would embrace homosexuality or support a pro-choice movement, the answer would have surely been a resounding, dogmatic "**NEVER!**" Tragically, it has happened in many instances.

Ask an evangelical or Pentecostal today if they believe that the authority of God's Word will ever be seriously questioned within their ranks. Most would declare it to be virtually impossible. But, even now there are telltale signs among us that not everyone would side with the reformers whose motto was *"Sola scriptura"* (Scripture alone.) Modern church history should present a solemn warning to us all!

NOTE: *Inerrancy is being challenged today in the name of good hermeneutics.*

NOTE: Having a dogma or creed on paper is no assurance that it will be preached or practiced.

NOTE: *Saying the right words without making the right choices will inevitably lead to a tragic spiritual disaster.*

Does it seem we are on a slippery slope by rather arrogantly ignoring the tear-stained pages of our wonderful spiritual heritage? How can we escape the trap of our own making? Before we can even hope to impact a self-centered culture our hearts must sob in shame and repentance. Did the apostle Peter not tell us, *"Judgment must begin at the house of God"* (1 Peter 4:17)? Our Lord's return will be for a pure Church—without spot or wrinkle, holy and without blemish (Ephesians 5:27).

I confess that my heart is heavy—for our failures and the dangerous *lukewarmness* of His church. Will you pause here with me quietly and allow the Holy Spirit to uncover the most private and obscure corners of our inner man?

• Misfits

Christians who are trying to fit into this world are uncomfortably miserable. It is worse than the proverbial rock in the shoe on a 10 mile hike. Jesus did not hold back the truth from His disciples. In the final discourse with them prior to the cross, He candidly said, *"If the world hate you, ye know that it hated me before it hated you. If ye were of the world, the world would love his own: but because ye are not of the world, but I have chosen you out of the world, therefore the world hateth you"* (John 15:18,19).

There is no such thing as nonoffensive Christianity.

My intentions are not to bring believers to a place of *despair*, rather to a place of *decision*. In many nations, those who declare their faith in Christ are in immediate danger and live with the possibility of death ever lurking near. We hear reports of those who have been willing to die for the cause of Christ and are deeply moved. It all seems so far away. In a pluralistic, postmodern culture who can say that those who stand for truth will not become the focus of a ferocious spiritual war that is already taking place? Can we sing it with conviction: Take this whole world, but give me Jesus, I won't turn back, I won't turn back?

EMBRACING THE TRUTH

1. *Holiness is God's plan.* Pray daily for strength to walk in the Spirit and crucify the flesh.

2. *Holiness is God's plan.* Learn to love the things that God loves and despise the things that God despises.

3. *Holiness is God's plan.* Understand that His high and holy purpose is for man's benefit and fulfillment in this life as well as in eternity.

4. *Holiness is God's plan.* Realize that our Lord's church is to be pure and holy. Daily soul searching and repentance are urgent matters for each individual, each local body of believers, and the Church worldwide.

5. *Holiness is God's plan.* Be prepared to walk uprightly before God and men, while humbly sharing the love and grace of God by both word and daily living.

6. *Holiness is God's plan.* Pray, pray, pray for the Church as we draw ever closer to the coming of the Lord.

1. Elton Trueblood, *The Company of the Committed* (New York, NY: Harper & Row, 1961).

CHAPTER FOUR

INDEPENDENCE IS PURE BONDAGE

*"How can any man believe a command?
Commands are to be obeyed, and until we
have obeyed them we have done exactly
nothing at all about them. And to have heard
them and not obeyed them is infinitely worse
than never to have heard them at all,
especially in the light of Christ's soon return
and the judgment to come."*

A.W. Tozer

Independence is not a scriptural concept for the true Church and its individual members. The most frequently employed analogy in God's Word defining or describing the Lord's church is the human body. And, we know that our bodies are not comprised of a multitude of independent organs. The millions of cells must all function in proper place and order. The dreaded word *cancer* indicates that certain cells have abandoned the normal patterns and have begun a destructive journey through the body. No organism can survive indefinitely unless its parts contribute to the health of the whole.

The truth that should leap out from the pages of holy writ in this regard is *interdependence*. The basic theme of books in the New Testament focus on this issue.

In the letters to the Ephesians and Colossians, Paul describes Christ as the **head** of the Church.

"And God placed all things under his feet and appointed him to be head over everything for the church, which is his body,

the fullness of him who fills everything in every way" (Ephesians 1:22, NIV).

"Instead, speaking the truth in love, we will in all things grow up into him who is the head, that is Christ. From him the whole body, joined and held together by every supporting ligament, grows and builds itself up in love, as each part does its work" (Ephesians 4:15,16, NIV).

"For the husband is the head of the wife as Christ is head of the church, his body, of which he is the savior" (Ephesians 5:23, NIV).

"And He (Christ) is the head of the body, the church" (Colossians 1:18, NIV).

"He [arrogant person] has lost connection with the head, from whom the whole body, supported and held together by its ligaments and sinews, grows as God causes it to grow" (Colossians 2:19, NIV).

Jesus taught His disciples this foundational principle. In one of His last discourses (John 15) with them prior to the cross, He said, "I am the vine; you are the branches." Five times Christ spoke of this relationship by telling these followers to "abide [remain] in me." The positive result was that they would "bear much fruit." Conversely, since a "branch cannot bear fruit of itself" it is soon "withered; and men gather them, and cast them into the fire, and they are burned."

• LESSONS FROM THE FARM

I had a unique privilege during my growing up years. We lived in the city, but I also spent a considerable amount of time in the "country." Most of my parents' family lived in a rural area, and several were farmers. So, quite early I experienced the demanding rigors of life on the farm. I "picked cotton," "pulled corn," (before the days of the modern equipment) baled hay and frequently did the multitude of chores associated with raising and caring for farm animals. Often working alongside migrant workers, I had a cross-cultural education long before it became a popular course for doctoral studies in major universities.

It does not take one long to learn some basic lessons in that setting. These *responsibilities* were both *ongoing* and *time sensitive*. Animals had to be cared for seven days each week. At the appropriate time crops had to be harvested without delay. *Commitment* was a way of life, regardless of how you felt or what the weather was like. *Interdependence was absolutely essential to survival.* Everyone had to do his/her part in sync with the daily schedule. Unfortunately, we have abandoned some of those valuable lessons as we shifted from an agricultural to an industrial and now a technological society.

Many homes today could be accurately characterized as permanent motels. The occupants are mobile and independent, with few collective responsibilities and even fewer sacrificial relationships. This is dramatically less than God's plan for the family.

As disconcerting as it is to read the statistics of marriages that end in divorce and the emotional trauma experienced not only by adults, but especially by young children who are forced to divide their affections, it is even more horrifying to realize that a similar scenario is also being played out among believers in many local congregations. Surely this must break the heart of our Heavenly Father.

• MY WAY OR I'M OUTTA' HERE

Having been involved in ministries that included traveling for many, many years, I have been in local churches all across this nation. From the tiny rural congregation to suburban megachurches, from the poorest inner-city fellowships to those of enormous affluence, I have shared the gospel message. This has brought us in contact with scores of pastors who have become close friends and dear brothers in the Lord. Listening to their hearts speak, I have often heard words of deep pain as they told of a good family or several families who decided that something was not to their personal liking, so they soon migrated to another church a short distance away. Generally speaking, there was no major crisis of doctrine or morality. Someone got their feelings hurt and they nursed the injury carefully until it was all consuming. Now, nothing done in the church was right. And so, off they go to the next stop until someone there offends them. How tragic that the Church must spend so much time trying to appease those who claim to know and love Christ that the lost often go unnoticed and unreached.

> *There comes the time when believers must be mature enough to become a blessing to others rather than always having to be coddled as babies with colic.*

• MY WAY OR YOU'RE OUTTA' HERE

Obviously, there are two sides to every coin. With tearful shame and regret, it must be admitted that some preachers are more independent than the "Lone Ranger." Pride and ego have driven some who are called of God to disregard those around them. The pastor is indeed foolish who abuses His God-given place of spiritual leadership.

Peter's admonition is valid today: *"Care for the flock of God entrusted to you. Watch over it willingly, not grudgingly—not for what you will get out of it, but because you are eager to serve God. Don't lord it over the people assigned to your care, but lead them by your good example"* (1 Peter 5:2,3, NLT). The pastor must be tied heart to heart with the congregations he serves. He may or may not be a powerful pulpiteer, but if he respects the unique place each individual has in the body of Christ, he will be quite effective.

There are various forms of church polity, with the basic forms being *congregational, presbyterian, espicopal* or some mixture of the three. Church politics (in the sense of power struggles, etc.) can become quite offensive, especially to young believers. It is the solemn responsibility of the leader to avoid and prevent (as much as is possible) such confusion within the body of believers. The spiritual leader does not always have to win. He or she may not have the final answer on every subject.

As a young pastor, I served a church that had been "split" (unfortunately, most churchgoers know this term) over a decision as to whether a 12' by 12' room should be carpeted. Some of those people were so hurt by unkind remarks that they left the church. To this day, they have never allowed themselves to be lovingly accepting of others.

Administrative procedures in the local church must never become the basis for fellowship among believers.

• EQUIPPING THE SAINTS

While some have found them to be helpful, it seems that the various methods of evaluating spiritual gifts have the potential of becoming somewhat ego altering. That is, one can become either discouraged or possessive by the abundance or lack of gifts that he/she possesses. Such comments may be an oversimplification; however, it is important to keep in focus that the personal work of the Holy Spirit, rather than personal interests or aptitude, is the baseline for effective service. We must never attempt to replace the process of divine selection with our skills or charisma. This, too, can become an act of independence. Regardless of one's chosen methodology to arrive at the proper conclusion, it is unquestionably the Lord's plan that every member of the body of Christ be a contributing member. We serve Him through serving others. This reinforces the idea of interdependence as a valid and important scriptural principle that must not be overlooked or abandoned today.

In his letter to the Ephesians, which emphasizes the Church as the body of Christ, Paul clearly articulates that the "gifts" of apostles, prophets, evangelists, pastors, and teachers have been placed in the Church *"to prepare God's people for works of service, so that the Body of Christ will be built up until we all reach unity in the faith and in the knowledge of the Son of God and becoming mature."* He concludes this passage by emphasizing, *"From Him the whole Body, joined and held together by every supporting ligament, grows and builds itself up in love, as each part does its work"* (emphasis mine) (Ephesians 4:12-16, NIV).

Perhaps this cultural spirit of independence has led to the gradual development of the "performer-audience" pattern (more will be said about this later) observed in many local churches today. This is not God's plan for worship or the development of mature saints. There were no spectators on the Day of Pentecost. The 120 were all involved in the experience of worship and infilling of the Spirit. Soon they were participants in sharing the Good News. These two—*worship* and *witness*—are inextricably linked together. Those who do not worship are not likely to witness and those who do not witness are not likely to worship.

• BELIEVERS WHO DON'T LIKE CHURCH?

In trying to encourage some infrequent attendees to be more faithful to church, you have surely encountered such arguments as, "There are too many hypocrites in the church," or "I can worship more comfortably at home by myself. I don't like crowds," or "Brother Radio/TV speaker provides for my spiritual life." It won't wash! The scripture is clear: *"Let us not give up meeting together, as some are in the habit of doing, but let us encourage one another—and all the more as you see the Day approaching"* (Hebrews 10:25, NIV). How true this is today as world events race toward the fulfillment of God's timetable for mankind.

Over the years, it has been my privilege to minister to a lovely congregation of believers in a extremely destitute inner-city area of a major metropolitan area. Many of these devoted followers of Christ have been saved and delivered from the worst kinds of bondage and sin. Some of them continue to live in difficult and dangerous environments. So, when they come to church, they are never in a hurry to leave. Literally, the house of God has become a sanctuary for them. And, the fellowship they experienced with others of *"like precious faith"* was not only a source of encouragement, but a powerful deterrent against surrendering to the relentless daily attacks of Satan.

In the 1970s, the church we were serving prayerfully determined it to be the Lord's plan to become heavily involved in a variety of media ministries as a means of evangelizing the city. The path that unfolded is a marvelous record of divine guidance and intervention. Eventually, this outreach grew so the TV ministry was on a network affiliate in prime time. For several months each broadcast was in a location other than the church (shopping mall, outdoor site, etc.). I was concerned that the unchurched might be turned off by another church service. However, after seeking the Lord's guidance, we determined that the next program would originate in the sanctuary on a Sunday evening. That telecast had one of the best responses of any program. Why? It later dawned on me that even those viewers at home or in motels wanted to worship with others. By the way, most Christian TV programs are presented with a "live" audience today. The explanation is quite simple. Man is created in the image of God, and in worship man is both an *extension* of His love and the *recipient* of His love.

The very nature of God bespeaks of loving fellowship. *Koinonia*—the Greek word used often in Christian circles—denotes partnership, the share which one has in anything, a participation, or fellowship recognized and enjoyed. The Church is at its highest moment when worshipping together in true fellowship.

• HOW INDEPENDENT ARE YOU?

Can you identify some manifestations of the cultural attitude of independence that have crept into the body of Christ? Let's examine a few.

1. Unwilling to make commitments
   The Christian education director often has a full-time job trying to secure and retain teachers and workers for Sunday School classes, children's ministries or any number

of strategic training ministries that develop mature disciples. One person even suggested that those who serve in this vital capacity should be named "Phil Slots." Where are those believers who have been in the church since childhood? The most common excuse is. "I don't have the time." Perhaps in many cases the underlying meaning is, "I don't want to make the commitment." Reality forces us to admit that we do have the time (and usually resources) for the things that are important to us.

For far too many Christians the church has become only a distant planet, rather than central to their universe. The twinkle of personal interests shines so brightly that spiritual matters often seem quite dim by comparison.

The Lord's work is not the sole responsibility of those who have been called into vocational Christian service. Tragically, many pastors are under intense pressure to personally direct a plethora of ministries in the local church because no one is willing to sacrificially commit to serving.

2. <u>Resentful of accountability to the church</u>
According to Peter Drucker, the megachurch is one of the major social phenomenons of the 20th century. In many ways the larger church is able to serve its membership more effectively and develop a sustained evangelistic outreach into the community. And, this is surely a wonderful blessing from the Lord. By reason of finances and personnel smaller congregations are frequently unable to provide similar ministries. The downside is that some choose a megachurch simply because they desire to be lost in the crowd. They don't want to be missed or questioned about their attendance. The child of God who shuns accountability is, at the least, spiritually immature; or, even worse, trying to cover something he or she does not want others to discover.

3. Personal preferences take precedence over service

   If you are a parent, you recall the dramatic adjustments
   you made to accommodate the demands of having a newborn in your home. A loving parent cannot imagine being
   angry and refusing to feed a hungry baby at 3 a.m. Or, who
   would allow a child to wear a dirty diaper all day because
   he/she did not like the smell and refused to change it? It
   arouses strong passions to think of such absurdity in natural life. Yet, there are believers, who could and should be
   mature spiritual leaders, who sit pouting on the pew simply because they don't like the way things are being done.
   Refusing to be an edifying member as a protest to a particular style or approach is prelude to spiritual disaster—
   yours and the people impacted by your actions. There are
   no perfect churches. Hang around a congregation or small
   group long enough (in some cases it may not require an
   extended period of time) and you will surely encounter
   expressions of human depravity. Lest we forget the obvious, the Church is made up of *imperfect saints*, who by the
   grace of God have been redeemed and are *in the process* of
   spiritual maturation. As diligently as we strive to become
   Christlike in every aspect of life, absolute perfection will
   never be possible until that day of eternal promotion into
   our Lord's presence.

4. Refusal to resolve conflicts scripturally

   The New Testament reveals a significant number of conflicts among believers. The Church was only a few weeks
   old when the Greek widows begin to complain that the
   Hebrew widows were receiving preferential treatment.
   Again, we are reminded that believers have not yet been
   perfected. Thankfully, the process is ongoing. Admit it.
   We all see things from our own perspective. Perhaps the
   adage is correct: "There are three sides to every story—
   your side, my side, and the correct side." But, as a child of

God, it is not always necessary to be right or to win. Pride—the spirit of independence—brings conflict. Unresolved conflict hinders, or even worse, brings death to spiritual life as bitterness and resentment grow. Humility, a gentle spirit, and the willingness to be wronged rather than bringing confusion is God's way. Swallow your pride. Make restitution. It is vital to a healthy Body.

5. <u>Stewardship is virtually non-existent</u>

The tithe (one-tenth of one's income) is taught in Scripture as belonging to God. Some immediately react that tithing was exclusively under the Law of Moses. While I disagree with such an interpretation of Scripture, that discussion must be postponed until another occasion. Suffice it to say that those who oppose God's minimum are usually not consistently supporting His work with their financial resources. "I can't afford to tithe or give to missions or the building fund, etc." is proclaiming "My personal priorities rank above the kingdom of God." Too harsh? I think not. Believers who refuse to honor the Almighty with their finances do not have an eternal view of earthly life and its fleeting possessions. Surely the worth of our salvation is greater than the paltry things of this world. Old-timers said that when people <u>really</u> got saved their experience traveled from head to heart and all the way to the pocketbook. The truth is that when financial stewardship is viewed as discretionary, it will be an act of the <u>emotion</u> rather than of the <u>will</u>.

6. <u>Determine standard of holiness syncretistically</u>

Webster's defines *syn-cre-tism* as "a combination, reconciliation, or coalescence of varying, often mutually opposed beliefs, principles, or practices, especially those of various religions, into a new conglomerate whole typically marked by internal inconsistencies." The pick-and-choose buffet style of obedience has become increasingly popular with this generation. Doctrinal truth (Scripture) is accepted or rejected at one's personal whims. This fits my lifestyle; this does not. If the Bible says, *"Thou shalt not,"* that is **exactly** what it means. If it says, *"Thou shalt,"* then that is **exactly** what it means. You do not even need to pray about some things. Culture has changed; God has not. Holiness is not optional. To be sure, it is not a dose of bad medicine He forces on us. Living according to His plan provides true inner joy and peace.

After only a surface evaluation, we can easily understand how the cause of Christ suffers by such independent attitudes. Clubs and societies often require more of their members than the average church does. Fast-food restaurants frequently have signs on their entrance requiring customers to wear shoes and shirts. Surely, saints of the Most High God cannot feel put upon to be participating members of the greatest enterprise on earth.

If this message produces personal conviction, repent before the Lord in humility. Our world must see, hear, and feel the passion we speak and live as followers of Christ. This is opportune moment for those who profess Christ as Savior to focus their highest level of energy in edifying His body and evangelizing this lost generation. Let the Church be the Church!

EMBRACING THE TRUTH

1. *Interdependence* rather than independence is the correct scriptural concept for the Church. Christ is the **HEAD**—we are His **BODY**. Without Christ there is no life in the body. Without Christ there is no Church.

2. Every member of the body has a valuable and important-function as part of the spiritual organism known as the Church. There is no such thing as an insignificant believer. The eternal reward of individual believers will be determined in light of that member's contribution to the whole.

3. Service in the Lord's church is never without personal sacrifice. Mature believers are willing to subjugate personal desires to guide less mature believers into spiritual growth and development.

4. Attitudes demanding that local church *polity, policy,* and *procedures* be synchronized with my personal thought processes lead to confusion and dissension. Administrative styles must never become the foundation upon which spiritual fellowship is either established or maintained.

CHAPTER FIVE

HIGH MAINTENANCE—*low productivity*

*"It is altogether the way we look at things
whether we think they are crosses or not. And
I am ashamed to think that any Christian
should ever put on a long face and shed tears
over doing a thing for Christ which a worldly
person would only be too glad to do for
money."*

Hannah Whitall Smith

The disciples asked the question, too. *"What's in this for us?"* (Matthew 19:27). Jesus quickly assured them of both temporal blessings and eternal reward, but then forcefully reminded them that God alone determines the "wages" we receive. The primary theme in the Parable of the Vineyard Workers (Matthew 20) is that the singular concern for the servant should be to fulfill the Master's call to service. Conversely, the strong emphasis is that we must not focus on the payment/reward.. God is always just and fair. He can be trusted to do what is right.

In a casual conversation with several leaders of a denominational missions board, the subject of candidates for missionary service surfaced. One by one these men expressed concern that several recent applicants seemed inordinately preoccupied with an extensive list of assurances they expected from the agency by making a commitment to long-term international ministry. Is such a response precipitated by cultural attitudes? What of those pioneers who sought only affirmation to fulfill a vision? Their passion for the lost compelled them to give up everything to share the life-giving message of Christ. Their passion could not be suppressed.

Oren Munger, who died at age 25 of malaria in Nicaragua, penned it so beautifully in his song, "The Vision."

"Take me Master, use me,
I am leaning on Thy breast,
All ambitions fast are dying,
From this pain now give me rest.
On the altar I have lain them,
Now to Thee I give my heart,
Fill me with the fire of vision,
Let my passion ne'er depart."

• MAKE ME FEEL GOOD ABOUT MYSELF

Every true believer cares deeply for those around him, to say nothing of his family and friends, who are in the grasp of destructive pain such as this generation is enduring. Make no mistake about it. We are witnessing the dastardly consequences of human depravity. *"All have sinned and come short of the glory of God"* (Romans 3:23). God's grace, available through the substitutionary sacrifice of Christ on the cross, is the only solution to this cancerous sin problem.

Yet, I fear lest the pendulum has once again swung too far in the noble desire to offer hope to those who are brutally ravished by the pain of personal circumstances. Hear my heart. Has the Church become an enabler for those who seek emotional security but are unwilling to respond to scriptural admonitions? For people to feel good about *"self"* a philosophy of self-acceptance has to be instilled in their minds. The *motivational sermons*, the *sound byte gospel*, the *psychological justification* for disobedience to the laws of God, feed the carnal nature. It is the flesh trying to be holy. It cannot work. I'm <u>NOT</u> OK—you're <u>NOT</u> OK. The cross of Christ is confrontational. Coming face to face with the guilt of personal sin is not pleasant. Remember, the father did not offer the prodigal a cleaner pigpen. God's grace is beyond comprehension. How He could love any of us can only be explained in Jesus. And, the marvelous truth is that God, for Christ's sake, has forgiven all our sins. The past has been cleansed by the blood of Jesus. Now, *"justified by faith," "there is no condemnation"* to the child of God. That is the way to feel good about yourself! Let His worthy Name be praised forever.

• COMPETE WITH MY WORLD

Do you have any silly fantasies? I have always wondered what it would be like to bring a person back to the present time who had been deceased for a hundred or more years. Imagine how dramatic the changes are that have occurred during that period. Having never known about TV, cell phones, computers, or a zillion other things that we depend on and take for granted every day, no doubt the person would be overwhelmed. Even for us who have lived through the process, the evolution of computer technology is mind-boggling. What is state of the art today is obsolete within weeks or months. I resisted the notion of naming some current technological phenomenon, knowing that, it too will be ancient history in a short time, and some reader would view it with the same humor that many of us recall the eight-track tape.

This generation is force-fed a constant diet of glitz and glitter through the most advanced forms of technology available at any given moment. Every form of media (and it does seem that some of them take on a life of their own) is incessantly vying for attention. Admittedly, the product can be quite compelling. Herein is the dilemma facing the Church. Anything not as fast paced tends to soon appear dull and boring. Anything less professionally produced seems hokey. Anything not in real-time (from the World Series to another war somewhere) seems like old news.

Now bring high-energy, every-minute-scheduled, financially conscious (either affluent or struggling), mobile, informed, stressed-out, and bone-weary people and plop them down in a church pew. Giving God an hour or two on Sunday morning is a major concession for the present world mindset. Outside of personally experiencing the awesome power of God, the mind can become easily frustrated or boredom can torment the mind. Mentally distracted by a score of other things—from the football game on TV at noon to the big sale at the mall—many sit in church counting the minutes until the benediction. So, the pastor, who can hardly find anyone to bear the weight of ministry with him, and the member, who attends simply out of family tradition or obligation, are both ready to toss in the towel.

Understand it clearly. The redemptive purposes of God must be the exclusive mission of the Church. While the scriptural outflow of His love has relational and societal implications, the Church must begin with matters of the spirit. (Man is first and foremost a spiritual being, made in the image of God.) The Church has a distinctively clear objective. There is no higher purpose than to prepare men and women for eternity. Attempts to compete with the world are not only a virtual impossibility for the Church; they are quite unnecessary. By the work of the Holy Spirit, not the ingenuity and cleverness of man, Christ is revealed as God's Son and our Savior. Please do not mistakenly construe these comments to imply that God approves of a sloppy, half-hearted, undisciplined approach to His work. Only our best is acceptable before Him.

Just a few hours before He went to the cross, Christ gave a solemn warning concerning preoccupation with the world in view of the coming day of divine judgment. *"But take heed to yourselves and be on guard lest your hearts be overburdened and depressed—weighed down—with the giddiness and headache and nausea of self-indulgence, drunkenness, and worldly worries and cares pertaining to (the business of) this life"* (Luke 21:34, Amplified).

No fingers are pointed at either pulpit or pew. God alone is the judge of all men. However, the hypnotic preoccupation with the present cannot be waved off as a non-issue. The apparently harmless advances of culture have done a real number on the Church.

> We long to be *entertained*, while God desires for us to be *humbled*. We struggle for cultural *acceptance*, while God is pleading for us to be *set apart*. We clamor for more *activity*, while God is longing for us to be content in *His presence*.

Do not be tricked by Satan into believing that God alone is not enough. Our best efforts are dismal failures, unless there is empowerment from above. Let the world race by at supersonic speed. The admonition of Scripture is still apropos—*"Be still and know that I am God"* (Psalm 46:10). Perhaps this would be an appropriate moment to lay this book aside and wait quietly in the Lord's presence. Allow Him to communicate with you. Listen to what He has to say. You will be blessed and refreshed.

• I'VE BEEN HURT

I was the speaker for a convention in Colorado Springs, Colorado, and the concluding evening service was a banquet. About 2,500 attendees were waiting to enter the large ballroom that night, so I was ushered around the back way through the kitchen. While waiting there, I spoke with the women who would be serving the meal. Learning that several were from other nations, I posed a favorite question: "What do you find different in the American culture from that of your own home?" Without hesitation, one of the women, in broken English, said emphatically, "In America, everyone wants to sue everyone else!" What a sad commentary for a nation that has been historically identified as Christian America.

At times methinks that the worst *cult* of this generation is what I have dubbed "The Cult of Pain." Everyone seems to have a grievance. Life has not been fair. My rights have been violated. Everything is bad and getting worse, and I want the whole world to know how rotten I have been treated. Angry and sullen, lashing out at the least provocation, such people can never be appeased and those around them are forced to walk on the proverbial eggshells. Sadly, many have carried this personal pain into the Church and have never allowed Christ to heal their broken, hurting hearts.

Some have encountered such deep emotional trauma that it sends shudders up the spine to think about it, let alone have to live in or through it. How much worse this has become in recent years with the breakdown of the scripturally defined family—one man married to one woman for life. As divorce and the number of dysfunctional families have escalated, so has the pain level of this generation. Talk to young people and you will find that many of them have been shuffled between parents and other family members, becoming pawns of the hatred that has developed between supposedly mature adults.

While this subject may seen ancillary, it is closely akin to the message of this book. Christians, by the thousands, even those who profess to be born again and attend church regularly, have been deceived by a cultural standard and have dissolved their marriages. Is it any wonder their children have difficulty in trying to sort out the reality of God? No, divorce is not an unpardonable sin; however, it need not even be an option for born-again believers. There should be no domestic disputes that are bigger than God's power to heal. And, those who serve Christ are certainly not following a pattern of unfaithfulness to their companion. A genuinely Christian home is possible when *both* husband and wife love Christ supremely and are willing to practice a godly lifestyle in private as well as in public.

Back to the subject at hand. While the Church is indeed to be a hospital for the hurting, it follows that the "patients" should begin to recover by the healing provision of Christ. If this is not happening, either the hospital is not functioning properly or the patient is refusing to accept treatment. Often an inordinate amount of the pastor's time is spent with a relatively small number of people. In some cases professional help is needed and the ministry of a Spirit-filled counselor who follows scriptural principles can be valuable both to the church and the individual. However, others are clinging to some negative experience (of years ago) and repeatedly want someone else to know and relive the pain they suffered. This incident has become a hedge of protection—an excuse for immature behavior.

I knew a woman who wept for years because her unsaved husband mistreated her because of her faith. The whole congregation was sympathetic with this saint who had to endure so much to serve Christ. Then one day the man found Christ. Shortly thereafter, she quit the church.

Our only child, Mischelle, died from a rare type of leukemia just a few days before her 11th birthday. Were those 16 months of her illness difficult? Words cannot describe the pain we experienced. What about now? All our lifelong friends are proudly showing pictures of their grandkids. Marcia and I will never have the joy of being grandparents. Why do I recount this personal experience? To solicit your sympathy? No, rather to declare that in spite of life's deeply painful and dark hours, God is always there to carry us through by His grace. It is His unfailing promise to those who trust in Him.

Fear questions if God will;
Doubt questions if God can.

God can and does bring deliverance. Ask the three Hebrew children. Ask Daniel. Ask the demoniac of Gadara. Ask Peter or Paul about prison. The power of the Word is incredible when life has swirled out of control. No commentary, no preacher or teacher—just the Word all by itself is one megadose of healing medicine. The Holy Spirit within consoles and comforts even when it appears that hell has been unleashed all around. The words of an old song come to mind: *Then trust alone the mighty God, He speaks the winds obey. Take courage then, oh fainting heart, for you He will make a way.* Victory is on the way!

• BY WHAT AUTHORITY

In a chapel service at the ministerial training college where I served for more than two decades, we invited a guest to make a presentation concerning *abortion*. It was excellent. He spoke of conception as the origin of life and included photographic illustrations of the developmental process of a fetus from the early weeks until maturity and birth. He also showed graphic scenes of actual abortion procedures. To say that it was quite sobering would be a dramatic understatement. When he finished, the student body gave him a standing ovation. He stood in awe and openly wept. Later he confided it was a rarity for this presentation to receive such acceptance. In the process of scheduling meetings in various churches, a significant number of the pastors he contacted refused to discuss the subject. Others indicated it was too controversial; others declared the whole idea as not being politically correct. Surprisingly, some pastors viewed abortion as a matter of choice rather than a moral issue.

Has the authority of God's Word been compromised by public opinion? Does the Church step into the shadows when there are issues that cut across the grain of culture? One has to wonder how many other principles of Scripture are being avoided or ignored for the sake of not offending anyone, or, worse, to maintain membership numbers and financial support.

The prophets of Old Testament vintage told it like it was. One can hardly read the prophetic books without feeling a need to go somewhere and repent. Their message was plain, direct, and spoke to the heart of the problem. For this strong declaration, *"Thus saith the Lord,"* many gave their lives.

As Jesus looked over the city of Jerusalem, He wept and spoke these passionate words. *"O Jerusalem, Jerusalem, you who kill the prophets and stone those sent to you, how often I have longed to gather your children together, as a hen gathers her chicks under her wings, but you were not willing!"* (Luke 13:14, NIV). Having publicly denounced King Herod's adulterous lifestyle, John the Baptist was beheaded

(Matthew 21:3-12). But the king was a pagan. Such a defensive, angry response was to be anticipated from an ungodly person (as well it might be today.) But the prophets were speaking to God's chosen people, who were a type of the New Testament church.

Have we become intoxicated with the wine of acceptance? Dare we slink away from our culture to avoid conflict? Is the fear of God's judgment simply a historic relic from past generations? God give us prophetic voices today who with *unflagging boldness, unquenchable passion, and unreserved compassion* declare the distinction between righteousness and evil. Men and women of God, called and anointed as His spokespersons, once again be sobered by this awesome responsibility. The word that came to Ezekiel, the prophet to the Jews in Babylonian captivity, resonates like a thunderous blast on a stormy night: *"Son of man, I have made thee a watchman unto the house of Israel: therefore hear the word at My mouth, and give them warning from Me."* God proceeds in this same chapter (Ezekiel 3) to tell Ezekiel that if he does not warn the people, their blood will be on his hands.

The message of the prophet Joel to *"blow the trumpet in Zion"* (Joel 2) was not to blast forth a sound of victory. Quite the opposite. God was calling for the deepest kind of contrition and repentance. So, it must be today. Sadly, some will not hear with open hearts and will be offended. But that does not change His Word.

• OFF THE BENCH—ONTO THE FIELD

The Holy Spirit has spoken personally to my heart. I feel a sense of deep conviction. What should I do to become a more productive member of our Lord's Church?

1. Immediately repent of any and all self-centered attitudes. Ask the Lord to show you specific areas that hinder your spiritual life. Perhaps you did not even realize they control a room in your heart.

2. Make restitution according to Scripture. It may be painful, but you will never make progress until you have taken this step of obedience.

3. Purpose in your heart to become a giver rather than a taker. Trust God to open the right doors for you to share your faith in meaningful ways. Remember, it may not be on the platform or in a public forum. Living for Christ is, as this generation says, 24-7—which means 24 hours a day, 7 days a week.

4. Become a true worshipper each time you enter the house of God. Listen for truth from the Word that is applicable to your present need.

5. Support the church and its delegated leadership. If doing so becomes an honest impossibility, then for your spiritual well-being locate a church that ministers to you. Become an active member and stay put!

6. Develop a network of fellow believers who stay in close communication and to whom you are willing to be accountable. Challenge each other to continue to grow in the Lord.

EMBRACING THE TRUTH

1. Believers are to *"count the cost"* of serving Christ; however, in comparison to the price He paid for our redemption, there is absolutely nothing we could do to ever earn or repay the gift of eternal life.

2. The world will constantly flash the best it has to offer before you. At times it will appear extremely appealing. Remember, the pleasures of this world are only temporary and will soon disappear, often leaving a carnage of human pain and sorrow in its wake.

3. Become an asset to your local church family. Don't expect others to carry your share of the load. Take the initiative in doing the menial tasks. Don't even expect to be recognized for your service.

4. Pray and believe for a powerful visitation of the Holy Spirit. There is nothing quite like a genuine revival to move the saints into action.

CHAPTER SIX

THE MISSING THREE Rs
Repentance, Reverence, Reconciliation

"Humility, the place of entire dependence on God, is, from the very nature of things, the first duty and the highest virtue of the creature, and the root of every virtue. Humility is the only soil in which the graces root; the lack of humility is the sufficient explanation of every defect and failure."

Andrew Murray

Back to basics. From the disappointed business executive to the frustrated football coach, the phrase is frequently employed. On one occasion Vince Lombardi, the inimitable, long time coach of the Green Bay Packers, stood in the locker room at halftime after a miserable performance by the team during the first thirty minutes of play, held a football in his hand and said, "Men, this is a football."

Looking back on my years growing up in church, I recall that almost every sermon had the same content—regardless of where the pastor took the text. Included were the four cardinal doctrines of our church. You could count on hearing about salvation, Holy Spirit baptism, divine healing, and the second coming of Christ. Those stalwart men and women of God may not have had the privilege of a formal education, but they knew what they believed. The enthusiastically repeated discourse of these basic scriptural truths laid a rock-solid foundation of faith in my life that holds firm to this very day.

When is the last time you heard a simple, basic presentation of the gospel? Has the Church been caught up in the social agenda of this generation? Are we more concerned about being accepted by society at large? Do we avoid certain spiritual and moral issues in order to avoid controversy? The apostle Paul solemnly warned to the believers in the region of Galatia not to abandon their foundational faith.

"Oh, foolish Galatians! Have you lost your senses? After starting your Christian lives in the Spirit, why are you now trying to become perfect by your own human effort?" (Galatians 3:1,3, NLT).

"Those who are trying to force you to be circumcised are doing it for just one reason. They don't want to be persecuted for teaching that the cross of Christ alone can save" (Galatians 6:12, NLT).

So how can we stop the erosion that is eating away at the spiritual life and health of many in our Lord's church? Can we see genuine revival today or must we simply wring our hands in despair? Let's go back to the beginning. Start at the starting point without looking for shortcuts and quick fixes. Forget about the drive-through lanes. Cling to the altar until the heavens are opened pouring forth the drought-ending rain. God will honor His Word. Revival with come.

REPENTANCE

"To repent is to alter one's way of looking at life; it is to take God's point of view instead of one's own."

Anonymous

One Sunday morning after preaching from the passage, *"Except ye repent, ye shall all likewise perish"* (Luke 13:3, 5), a high-ranking leader in a well-known Bible distribution organization came to me. "This is the first time anyone told me that I needed to repent," he sobbed. How tragic that week after week both sinner and saint occupy church pews and are never told they must repent. The message of grace must be balanced with the warning of God's judgment upon those who do not repent. Yes, it is still black and white—heaven or hell. According to Scripture, you are either saved or lost.

Repentance is basic. Our *justification* is contingent on it. Our *sanctification* is dependent on it. There is no resurrected life without first being *forgiven of sin*. This does not just encompass being sorry that our sins were discovered. Repentance is incomplete without the dimension of *"go and sin no more."* It is a two-step process: **turning from sin** and **turning to God**.

REPENTANCE IS NOT ONLY NECESSARY FOR THE SINNER TO BECOME A SAINT;
IT IS ALSO NECESSARY FOR THE SAINT WHO HAS BECOME A SINNER.

The **prophets** were raised up by God to preach repentance to His chosen people. Read the prophetic books of the Old Testament, and you will be captured by the strong language they used. Their message was not about a Sunday afternoon stroll in the park.

John the Baptist, unconventional, but anointed by God, preached a powerful message of repentance. His generation came en masse to hear him and were cut to the heart by his straight-forward preaching.

Jesus preached love and forgiveness, but He cut no slack for the self-righteous religious leaders who had impure hearts. He even told them that "tax collectors and harlots" would get into heaven before they did.

The New Testament (other than the Gospels and Acts) was written specifically to followers of Christ. Yet, **Paul**, **Peter**, **James**, **John**, and **Jude** all presented clear instruction on the nature and importance of repentance.

In the Book of Revelation (Chapters 2,3), Christ has a message to each of the seven churches in Asia Minor. Listen to what He had to say to them.

Ephesus   *"repent and do thy first works"*

Pergamos   *"repent or else"*

Thyatira   *"I will cast them into great tribulation, except they repent"*

Sardis   *"I have not found thy works perfect before God. . .remember therefore, and hold fast, and repent"*

Laodicea   *"be zealous therefore, and repent"*

Only the churches at Smyrna and Philadelphia were not urged to repent of wrongdoing.

• How many times do we repent?

Again, in 1 John, the beloved apostle writing under the Spirit's inspiration forwards this letter to the Church in general, as there is no specific person or group to whom it is addressed. The instruction he gives is appropriate for our time, as it was for the first century.

"If we claim to be without sin, we deceive ourselves and the truth is not in us. If we confess our sins, he is faithful and just and will forgive our sins and purify us from all unrighteousness. My dear children, I write this to you so that you will not sin. But if anybody does sin, we have one who speaks to the Father in our defense—Jesus Christ, the Righteous One" (1 John 1:8,9; 2:1, NIV).

Paul admonished the Romans not to assume it was acceptable to sin—just to show how wonderful the grace of God was (Romans 6). The obvious answer to the question, "How often do we repent?" is "As often as we need to." Although we are in the daily process of maturing spiritually, please understand that it is not necessary for a believer to sin every day. While none of us will ever reach absolute perfection in this present life, by the grace of God we sin less and less as we take on the image of Jesus Christ. Nonetheless, a spirit of true repentance should prevail in our hearts day and night. This must be more than a perfunctory "Now I Lay Me Down to Sleep" type prayer. Our unworthiness in the light of His sacrifice will keep us ever at the foot of the Cross.

In citing a few of the more prominent and prevalent sins that we must acknowledge in this generation, this is by no means intended either as an inclusive or exclusive list. Ask the Holy Spirit to turn a bright, searching spotlight into the most remote corner of your heart. If you are truly sincere, He will reveal those secret or hidden areas that need to come under the cleansing blood of Christ.

Pride. God hates it. Careful now. If you boldly declare that you have no pride, it could well be that Satan has camouflaged it beneath a whole forest of good deeds and sacrificial service. According to Scripture, improper motivation lurks dangerously near all the time. In the Sermon on the Mount, Jesus spoke of those who performed religious activities for recognition. His conclusion was, *"This is all the reward they will ever get"* (Matthew 6:5, NLT).

Self-sufficiency is a mockery to God. If it were possible for man to control his own destiny, there would be no need for a Supreme Being. The undeniable fact is that we are *depraved*. Theologians debate whether we are sinners because of Adam's sin or because of personal sin. The answer seems relatively simple. One is not mutually exclusive of the other. As a direct result of the first man's disobedience, all his descendants have a bent toward evil. So while Adam brought sin into this world, the rest of us (except for Christ) have perpetuated evil. Romans 3:23 drops us all in the same pit. *"For all have sinned, and come short of the glory of God."* All the combined efforts that fallen man can muster are pitifully helpless to change our nature.

God is indeed my friend,
but I am not His equal.
There can only be one God.

An unforgiving spirit prevents the disbursement of divine forgiveness. This is really serious. If we refuse to forgive another person, God will refuse to forgive us. Jesus could not say it any stronger than He did. When Peter asked the Lord how many times he should forgive someone who sinned against him, he thought it munificent in suggesting seven times. Jesus burst his bubble when He told him to forgive *"seventy times seven."* After telling a story that could leave no room for misunderstanding as to what He meant about the importance of forgiving another equal, Jesus said, *"This is* how my heavenly Father will treat each of you unless you forgive your brother from your heart" (Matthew 18:35, NIV). Resentment and bitterness will destroy you spiritually. Repent and the Lord will purify your spirit and mind.

Lack of compassion for the lost negates the very reason for the Church. People all around us are blinded by the deceitfulness of Satan and sin. People, in every nation desperately need to hear the message of eternal life in Christ. Let it be heralded from the lips of every born-again believer— Jesus Christ is the only way to salvation. What about your own family? When is the last time you wept for them? What about the poor? What about the rich? Your neighbors, the people you work with, and on and on the list could go, are headed for eternal damnation unless they meet the Master. Surely the Church must repent of being content with "our four and no more" for such a long time. Time is short. We must seize the moment before it is too late.

Personal sins for which you have not repented are repulsive to a holy God. It will grow like a cancer until it cuts off the life-giving supply of divine mercy and grace. The good news is that when we come to Christ pleading for forgiveness, He removes the guilt and condemnation (Romans 8:1) and brings us into right relationship with the Father (2 Corinthians 5:19). However, the same Word of God that promises forgiveness also warns against attempting to "hide" or "cover" sin. Sins of immorality are so prevalent today. Fornication, adultery, homosexuality, pornography are viewed as the normal, accepted pattern of life. Young people often seem surprised upon hearing the standard of purity that a holy God established for human relationships. Don't be deceived by a self-justifying culture. God has not changed His mind. Our bodies are the *"temple of the Holy Spirit"* (1 Corinthians 6:19).

emonial observances under the old covenant, the
ble fact is that God desired a submissive heart. *He
lowship with His people far more than He wanted their*
At times, God rejected the sacrifices because the one
g the sacrifice had an impure heart.

nimals offered for sacrifice had to be the best that the
ad. No crippled, blind, or deformed lamb would
And, by the way, every person was required to bring
g, no matter how meager. All of this was for the
of teaching the Children of Israel reverence.

oes this flesh out under the new covenant of grace.
lustrate. If I were called to meet with some govern-
nitary, I would show him or her respect by being
ately dressed for the occasion. Of course, such an
s superfluous. Who can in any wise be compared to
nd only Creator God? (Read Isaiah 40. You will be
Here are a few simple guidelines for what is appro-
ire in the God's house in any generation.

st
gain, Spirit-filled believers will have no desire to
another to be distracted by that which is suggestive
sual. The Holy Spirit will guide you. Be careful, as
is such an onslaught of the vulgar and cheap (TV,
s, music, etc.) that one can quickly be desensitized
at is wholesome and pure in the sight of God. The
ling styles of clothing in contemporary culture will
be an acceptable model.

extremes
d standard to consider is how such attire is judged by
people. Those who have been down the road a few
have the advantage of looking in both directions.

Perhaps the Holy Spirit has spoken to your heart concerning one of these sins or another not identified here, and you have felt conviction. That is good. He cares enough about you to show you the right way. Right now, while you are sensitive to His voice, why not find a private place and empty yourself before Him. It will be one of the most memorable moments in your spiritual journey.

REVERENCE

"Worship is to feel in your heart and express in some appropriate manner a humbling but delightful sense of admiring awe and astonished wonder and overpowering love in the presence of that most ancient Mystery, that Majesty which philosophers call the First Cause but which we call Our Father Which Art in Heaven."

A.W. Tozer

"Is *nothing* sacred anymore?" we are prone to ask when a cultural tradition of long standing is debunked. As time passes and a new generation comes along, often the significance of the past is lost in the dusty pages of history. With the advent of modern media technology and real-time news, life is as up to date as the latest crime or war. Even the events of last week may seem a long time ago. Consequently, it should not be shocking when the scripturally based practices of the Church are cast aside without even a second glance. Among a big collection of antiques stored in the attic can be found *reverence*. From discussions approving being angry with God all the way to dress in the house of worship that is commensurate with an overnight camping trip, God is sort of taken for granted. What a tragedy.

• It's smart to be reverent

The Word of God has a great deal to say about the *"fear"* of the Lord. The meaning is *"reverence,"* a solemn recognition of His power and authority. After all, He is the Creator—Giver and Sustainer of life. It is beyond ridiculous to stand toe-to-toe with Him, demanding our own rights or to act as if He has no authority in our lives.

The prophet Jeremiah received an illustrated lesson at the potter's house. *"So I went down to the potter's house, and I saw him working at the wheel. But the pot he was shaping from the clay was marred in his hands; so the potter formed it into another pot, shaping it as it seemed best to him. Then the word of the Lord came to me: 'O house of Israel, can I not do with you as this potter does?' declares the Lord. 'Like clay in the hand of the potter, so are you in my hand, O house of Israel'"* (Jeremiah 18:3-6, NIV).

Paul reiterated this truth to the Roman believers. *"But who are you, O man, to talk back to God? Shall what is formed say to him who formed it, 'Why did you make me like this?' Does not the potter have the right to make out of the same lump of clay some pottery for noble purposes and some for common use?"* (Romans 9:20,21, NIV).

Examine a few of the scripturally promised benefits. *"Reverence for the Lord is the foundation of true wisdom"* (Psalm 111:10, NLT).

"The fear of the Lord. . .
prolongeth life"	(Proverbs 10:27).
is a strong confidence"	(Proverbs 14:26).
is a fountain of life"	(Proverbs 14:27).
tendeth to life"	(Proverbs 19:23).

• Only the best

Based on scriptural record, I have ad the manner in which we present oursel worship is an expression of reverence. ticipants in a church service appear as i ballgame. Shorts (both men and wome tank tops, shoes untied, cap on backwa the back of the chair or pew may a fi more than the style of the moment. Bu

The immediate rejoinder is that yo *"outward appearance"* and God is not i look like, because He *"looks on the hea* is no indication that the verse being qu do with manner of dress. Read the s However, the truth is that *God does look* exactly the point to be considered. Ar presence of the Almighty, Eternal God c out with our buddies? This can be car either direction. Please understand that anywhere and at any time, and He is alw do so. Also, I am certain that God is checking suit labels as we enter into th narrow the discussion to (1) the corpc and (2) coming before Him in a manne ence and respect.

Old Testament patterns speak volur Coming into God's presence was a frightl Mount Sinai to the tabernacle in the wilc ly in the beautiful temple that Solomon b before Jehovah with fear and trembling. to purify himself before entering into the privilege we enjoy because of Christ).

many
undisp
wanted
sacrific
presen

The
person
qualify
sometl
purpos

Hov
Let me
ment c
approp
analog
the on
blessec
priate

1. Moc
Borr
caus
or s
ther
mov
to w
prev
harc

2. Avo
A gc
godl
mile

Hindsight is a marvelous instructor. Listen to what they have to say. As an illustration: Is brightly colored hair, dark side Gothic look clothing with ear, eye, lip, tongue, eyebrow and various other body rings considered every-day, normal dress? A believer does not ever want to negate his testimony by appearing to company with those openly rebellious to the principles of moral conduct. Not sur-prisingly, people who have been delivered from such a lifestyle want to avoid it completely and often have little tolerance for professing Christians who participate in it.

3. **Appropriate for the occasion**
   For those who are leading others into worship, take extreme care not to call attention to yourself by the man-ner in which you are dressed. Did you ever notice that Jesus was not criticized for His dress? If there had been any possibility of doing so, the religious leaders would have taken Him to task.

With such a low level of respect for authority in the home, business and political worlds, and (unfortunately) the church, it is imperative we return to humbly reverencing God in every aspect of life. *Among the many benefits and bless-ings of genuine revival one will surely be a renewed emphasis on reverence.*

RECONCILIATION

"The truly humble person will not only look admirably at the strengths of others, but will also look with great forgiveness upon the weaknesses of others."

Jeremy Taylor

In recent years a new awareness of the need for reconciliation in the Church in general has begun to develop. People who have experienced or caused deep hurt are openly confessing before each other and asking for forgiveness. In a new way, the Church is seeing its mission to evangelize the lost and have turned from some of the petty differences that have kept those who are in Christ apart. My prayer is that by the grace of God it will be possible to close the door on what happened in the past and get on with the business of reaching this world for Christ while there is yet time.

Because of space limitations, our comments will be restricted to the need for reconciliation among individual believers in a local body.

• Conflict is a reality

Reading the Scriptures, you need go only as far as Genesis 4 to find conflict (**Cain** killed his brother **Abel**.) The herdsmen of **Abraham** and **Lot** feuded over the best pasture for their flocks and herds (Genesis 13). Who can forget the conflict between **Jacob** and **Esau** (Genesis 27) or that son **Absalom** tried to usurp the throne from his father, **King David** (2 Samuel 14,15).

The Spirit-filled New Testament church experienced conflict among godly people. (The Bible does not shield us from reality.) There was a dispute between the **Greek** and **Hebrew** widows (Acts 6) over who was receiving the best treatment. **Paul** and **Barnabas** had *"sharp contention"* between them over John Mark (Acts 15). Paul urged **Euodias** and **Syntyche**, who were good workers, to settle their conflict (Philippians 4:2,3). Even John the beloved identified **Diotrephes** as one who *"loved to have preeminence"* in the church (3 John, verse 9).

People have different *opinions.* People have different *personalities.* People have different experiences. Mix these together and the likelihood of conflict is strong—even among Christians. Then, the issue is not if conflict comes, rather how do we deal with it when it does come. The Scriptures are clear. In Matthew 18, a three-step pattern is established. First, go privately to the person. Second, if the conflict is not resolved by the two individuals, take two or three others with you to meet with the person. Finally, if both of these attempts have been unsuccessful, the matter should be taken before the church body. Here, only the first, *"just between the two of you,"* will be considered.

The scriptural injunction is, *"Do your part to live in peace with everyone, as much as possible"* (Romans 12:18, NLT). This requires constant diligence and even willingness to be wronged without yielding to the temptation to retaliate. In the Beatitudes Jesus taught the importance of living in peace. *"Blessed are the peacemakers: for they shall be called the children of God"* (Matthew 5:9). The Amplified version strengthens the meaning by adding, *"makers and maintainers"* of peace. Many hurtful conflicts could be avoided if one party refused to join the fray. It is rather difficult for a one-sided battle to take place.

The implication of the verse in Romans is that even when a person sincerely endeavors to be in a peaceful relationship with another, it may not always be possible to avoid conflict. What steps should you follow in facing this challenge?
1. Pray for divine wisdom.
2. Do not rush in to straighten the person out.
3. As much as possible, find out the facts. Never act on a rumor. The "he said/she said" game can be wicked.
4. Meet with the person in the most nonthreatening situation possible.

5. Do not accuse. Be gentle and loving so that you will have no regrets.
6. Be willing to accept the blame—even if you are absolutely certain your actions and motivation were pure.
7. Pray with the person and then forget that it ever happened—even if the other person does not.

The flow of the Spirit is hindered by bitterness and resentment toward a person of *"like precious faith."* Having listened to countless crushed hearts pour out stories of bruised and broken relationships, it is my conclusion that unresolved conflict between people who sit in the same sanctuary for worship week after week is one of the major hindrances to a spiritual breakthrough in many assemblies.

Finally, look at one of the lessons that Christ taught (by example) His disciples just before He went to the cross. The debate among the Twelve had to do with position and prominence. It was the subject of conversation among them frequently. On the eve of the Passover (compare Luke 22:24 and John 13:1-17), Jesus washed the disciples' feet. He explained the meaning of true servanthood: *"I have set you an example that you should do as I have done for you. I tell you the truth, no servant is greater than his master, nor is the messenger greater than the one who sent him"* (John 13:15,16, NIV). He added, *"A new command I give you: Love one another. As I have loved you, so you must love one another. By this all men will know that you are My disciples, if you love one another"* (John 13:34,35, NIV). Those who see this kind of relationship will be duly impressed by genuine respect and love among peers, rather than by self-centered scratching and clawing to climb to the top. Can we see it? Harmony among Christians is for more than personal tranquillity—it is the testimony to a confused, self-centered world that Jesus really does make a difference in our behavior.

EMBRACING THE TRUTH

1. **Repentance** is not only necessary for the initial salvation experience; it is important for every believer to maintain a humble, contrite spirit before Almighty God.

2. **Repentance** is always a prerequisite for genuine revival in the Church. God does not wink at sin in any individual.

3. **Reverence** before the Creator God should never be deemed as cruel slavery. Rather, to be allowed into His hallowed presence is the greatest privilege that will ever be afforded to any human being.

4. **Reverence** in corporate worship settings should always be expressed in a manner that is appropriate and will bring glory and honor to His holy name. Believers should never engage in any activity that would distract or discourage others from worship.

5. **Reconciliation** between two believers whose relationship has been damaged or destroyed is evidence of the work of grace in their lives. The initial step in the scriptural procedure for reconciliation must be prayerfully obeyed.

6. **Reconciliation** which produces genuine respect and love, even though each individual personality is unique, is a powerful testimony to the unsaved. Love among believers is a major attraction to those who are suffering the pain of damaged or broken relationships.

CHAPTER SEVEN

THE GOSPEL OF WHAT'S HAPPENING

"It appears that too many Christians want to enjoy the thrill of feeling right, but are not willing to endure the inconvenience of being right."

A.W. Tozer

He bounded onto the platform dressed in black—tight body shirt, even tighter leather pants, knee-high boots—with his waist-long blond hair in a pony-tail—and shouted into the microphone, "Let's have some church!" For the next 45 minutes he worked the crowd into an emotional frenzy, frequently employing such phrases as, "God just showed up!" The deafening music and incessant repetition of a few lyrics sounded eerily like a rock concert. Just as suddenly as he came, he was off the platform and out the side door. He was finished for the evening. The congregation—some frustrated, others exhausted—slumped into their pews, hardly ready to receive the Word of God with eager, open hearts.

An extreme situation? Surely. Nonetheless it illustrates how some have integrated cultural patterns into the worship experience. How tragic to sacrifice the awesome beauty of reverent worship for an emotional rush that tends to gratify the flesh more than to ascribe glory to the eternally holy God. There should be joyous liberty in the worship of our Redeemer. One common response during periods of revival in any generation has been the enthusiastic singing and spontaneous praise. There was no need for hype or cheerleading for these saints. Their rejoicing overflowed from hearts that simply could not contain the blessings of God. It happened at Pentecost and it has been happening ever since.

I was challenged by a pastor as being opposed to revival—to use his expression, "not in the river"—because we continued to used hymnbooks in our worship services. When I asked him how it was different to hold the words in our hands or to read them from a screen, he emphatically declared using hymnals "was not where God was moving today." Such attitudes must grieve the heart of our Father. How tragic to define worship in matters of personal choice and become judgmental of others who do not conform to that particular pattern.

Perhaps I should share a bit of my personal church background. I grew up in a Pentecostal church and have been preaching now for more than 40 years. What may be termed an emotional worship style has been a delightful part of my experience since childhood. Beginning in the ministry while still a teenager, I started as an evangelist—perhaps more appropriately titled as a revivalist. Although the Lord has afforded us choice opportunities in both pastoral and administrative responsibilities, I have never strayed away from those formative years. The passion to see the Lord's Church in *proper relationship* with Him and *powerful representation* of Him provides boldness in this attempt to speak to cultural influences that negatively impact God's people today. I continually pray that God will raise up many prophetic voices to uncompromisingly speak the Word of truth to this generation. The coming of the Lord is near; His church must be pure and holy.

True worship will always evoke some type of emotional response. Granted, it will not be the same for every individual, nor will an individual always respond in exactly the same manner. But the emotions (as well as the intellect and the will) will be impacted when one is truly praising and worshipping God. It is **scriptural**. Perhaps a study of the many scriptural expressions (i.e., singing, shouting, clapping, etc.) of worship would provide encouragement to the timid. Don't allow others to intimidate you. Just be positive He is the object of your worship.

Emotion in worship is **historical**. And, that includes many communions, not just the classic Pentecostals and contemporary charismatic believers. Pick up a volume on the Great Awakening. Read of revivals during the times of the Wesley brothers, Finney, Moody and other notable spiritual leaders. People were moved by the Spirit. First came deep conviction, then repentance, and finally great joy.

It is also to be **eternal**. Can you imagine not having any emotion when you stand in the presence of our Lord and Savior? The ultimate desire for every redeemed saint of God is to bow in the presence of the Savior and bless His name. If believers are unnerved by a little noise in church services, they may become quite uncomfortable at what will take place around the Throne of God. When our minds and hearts exalt the Almighty, we enjoy the most uniquely wonderful experience any human can ever hope to have in this present mortal state.

• SCRIPTURAL MANIFESTATION OR HUMAN RESPONSE?

The Old Testament provides visible examples of manifestations of God's presence and power when the people of Israel were corporately gathered before Him.

When Moses was on the mount, the people at the foot of the mountain saw God's presence. *"And the glory of the Lord abode upon Mount Sinai...and the sight of the glory of the Lord was like devouring fire on the top of the mount in the eyes of the children of Israel"* (Exodus 24:16,17).

When the tabernacle in the wilderness was completed and furnished according to the Lord's instructions, His glory appeared. *"Then a cloud covered the tent of the congregation, and the glory of the Lord filled the Tabernacle. And Moses was not able to enter into the tent of the congregation, because the cloud abode thereon, and the glory of the Lord filled the Tabernacle"* (Exodus 40:34,35).

What a magnificent demonstration of God's approval and presence at the dedication of Solomon's temple. *"And it came to pass, when the priests were come out of the holy place, that the cloud filled the house of the Lord, so that the priests could not stand to minister because of the cloud: for the glory of the Lord filled the house of the Lord"* (1 Kings 8:10,11).

God's presence was also revealed to individuals in the Old Testament record. In a time of discouragement, the prophet Elijah stood before the Lord on Mount Horeb. Remember, just days earlier, he had called down fire from heaven that had *"consumed the burnt sacrifice, and the wood, and the stones, and the dust, and licked up the water that was in the trench"* (1 Kings 18:38). This display of God's power had turned the hearts of the people back to God and the false prophets of Baal were put to death (1 Kings 18:40). Now at the mouth of the cave, there were divine manifestations of *strong wind*, *earthquake*, and *fire*. Elijah recognized these expressions of the power of God; however, on this occasion, He did not speak through them. Rather, the prophet heard *"a still small voice"* (1 Kings 19:11,12) giving him direction and encouragement for the future.

Every student of the Word has sensed the sacred moment in the life of Isaiah the prophet when he saw a vision of the throne of God (Isaiah 6). The experience changed his life and ministry dramatically. In Chapter 5 he pronounces *"woes"* (six times) upon the disobedient people of Israel. Then, in Chapter 6 he cries, *"Woe is me!"* Look quickly at Chapter 7:14 as the renewed Isaiah speaks prophetically concerning the coming Christ: *"Therefore the Lord himself shall give you a sign; Behold, a virgin shall conceive, and bear a son, and shall call his name Immanuel."* To this day Isaiah is known as the Messianic prophet. He had encountered the presence of the living God. Every message of warning and judgment ends with a message of hope for those who hear the voice of God and repent.

The vast array of <u>miracles</u> recorded in both Old and New Testaments reveal the power of God. This would include not only physical healings, but also provisions of food or protection in times of danger. The lengthy list presents a God who is concerned with every aspect of life. Specifically, divine healing is included in the atoning provision of the suffering and death of Christ. There is no scriptural indication such miracles have ceased today. If you have a physical illness or disease, as a child of God you can receive healing through Christ. He is still the great Physician. Why not pause at this moment and cry out to Him for your healing? This could be His exact timing to answer your prayer.

The New Testament record of Pentecost identifies the specific manifestation as *"speaking with other tongues, as the Spirit gave them utterance"* (Acts 2:4). However, there was also *"a sound from heaven as of a rushing mighty wind"* and *"there appeared unto them cloven tongues like as of fire, and it sat on each of them"* (Acts 2:2,3). Why did these two Old Testament manifestations of God's presence appear now? It was verification to these 120 believers that this new experience was indeed from God. We have the benefit of 2,000 years of history plus the written Word. They had neither. This had never happened previously. They, and subsequent believers who are part of the Church, were being filled with the Spirit's power to boldly declare that Jesus Christ is the Son of God and the only way to receive eternal life.

Unfortunately, some in the Church today downplay the urgency of being filled with the Spirit. Human intellect, acquired leadership skills, and appropriate relationships should not be minimized. However, they are not, nor can they ever become, replacements for the personal indwelling of the Holy Spirit. Perhaps the doctrinal position of your denomination or fellowship has prejudiced your mind against the present-day work of the Spirit in your life and in the Church. Let's not debate. Rather, will you carefully and prayerfully study what the Word has to say? Ask the Lord to show you personally through the Scriptures His plan and purpose for the Church today and how it is to be accomplished. Then, consider your place of service to the Master and how you can fulfill His will. If you are an earnest seeker, the Holy Spirit will illuminate the Word and provide personal application for your life.

> THE MINISTRY OF THE HOLY SPIRIT IS TO EXALT CHRIST. ANY SPIRIT THAT DOES OTHERWISE IS NOT FROM GOD. THE CENTRAL FOCUS OF EVERY ACTIVITY IN A SPIRIT-FILLED CHURCH WILL BE TO HONOR THE LORD JESUS CHRIST.

In reading the Scriptures (or hearing sermons), most have discovered the list of *"gifts"* or manifestations of the Spirit (1 Corinthians 12), as well as the *"fruit"* of the Spirit (Galatians 5). Some have tried to weigh these against each other. This is often done in noting the imperfections in the life of one who claims to be used by the Spirit in ministry gifts. While it is essential for every believer to walk uprightly and in close fellowship with the Lord, the undeniable truth is there are no perfect saints. The bumper sticker is correct: *"Christians aren't perfect—just forgiven."* Please understand that it is not an *either/or*; it is an *and/both*. The work of the Spirit is not compartmentalized. When given opportunity, the third person of the Trinity will enable us to *"walk in the Spirit"* (Galatians 5:16,25). When given opportunity, this same Spirit will *"give them* (supernatural manifestations) *to each one, just as he determines"* (1 Corinthians 12:11, NIV).

Since this volume is not intended as a study of doctrine, comments concerning the *"gifts of the Spirit"* will be abbreviated. However, a few axioms will be helpful in our consideration of this relevant subject.

GIFTS OF THE SPIRIT—1 CORINTHIANS 12

Gifts of <u>revelation</u>	**Word of wisdom**
	Word of knowledge
	Discerning of spirits
Gifts of <u>power</u>	**Faith**
	Working of miracles
	Healings
Gifts of <u>utterance</u>	**Prophecy**
	Tongues
	Interpretation of tongues

---

1. The gifts of the Spirit (1 Corinthians 12) are **resident within the Spirit**; the Spirit is resident within the believer.

2. **Any Spirit-filled believer may be used by the Spirit** as the vessel of choice on a given occasion.

3. **The Spirit selects the occasion and vessel** to be used for any supernatural manifestation.

ly (honestly) *seek to determine what is scrip-* what is the church culture of the moment. ...er that personal preferences can often hinder ...mind to a genuine move of the Spirit. Examine ...art to be certain you are earnestly seeking to ...e fullness of God's blessing. Revival is exactly ...reviving" of that which has been dormant. At ...must be acknowledged that the traditional way ...things could be changed for the better.

...th the style of worship, *consider the place of* ...*rd in worship.* What about the doctrinal posi... the Scriptures held as the highest authority for ...h and practice? Are believers maturing in the ...is celebration given precedent over preaching?

...h is the leadership accountable? How would it ...ed if you expressed honest and sincere concern ...me unusual doctrine or worship styles? This is ...ply that a disgruntled person should be given ...nce to find fault with everything leadership is ...emember, how God judged Korah for his attack ...Moses (Numbers 16).

...e three important questions:
...*he lost coming to Christ?*
...*elievers being discipled?*
...*the ministry have a worldview?*

...consider your own spiritual well-being. If you ...enthusiastically participate in a particular local ...ip, then search for a Bible-believing church that ...he Word and exalts Christ in joyful worship.

---

4. **Believers do not possess (own) rights to any gift.**

5. **The gifts are normally manifested within the assembled body of believers.** The group may not necessarily be large or meeting for a scheduled worship service in the sanctuary.

6. **The gifts of the Spirit should never be categorized.** That is, one is not more or less significant than the others. Nor should it be assumed that some are valid today while others were only for another period in church history.

This, in summary, attempts to identify the scriptural expressions of manifestations in both testaments. As you study the Word in depth, there will be irrefutable evidence that the glory of God is inextricably entwined with the person and work of the Holy Spirit. The New Testament church was and is a Spirit-filled church.

Now, how do we sort out the human responses in worship? Which are biblical? Which are personal expressions of an individual? Which are beyond the realm of genuine worship? A qualifying statement to guide us is needed at this point.

1. <u>Maintaining objectivity is often difficult.</u> Our preferences tend to color our perspective. That can easily lead to conclusions that are personality oriented, rather than scripturally founded.

2. <u>The Bible affords latitude in styles of worship.</u> It is often silent on the subject, especially in the New Testament. Having traveled into numerous cultural settings around the world, I discover that spiritually mature people approach worship in different ways. Who can determine that one is correct and the other is not?

3. <u>A serious breach in the unity of the body of Christ comes when certain responses in worship are viewed as the only way</u> by which it is possible to enter into God's presence. Perhaps this attitude is the most harmful distraction to the moving of the Spirit during times of special visitation and renewal. Those who demand and those who refuse must equally share in the blame. Satan is always pleased to blur our vision of Christ.

4. Prayerful caution must prevail so that a genuine **_manifestation_** does not devolve into a habitual **_method_**. Sadly, when this happens what began in reality eventually falls into the carnal pit of **_human manipulation_**.

• WHAT SHOULD I AVOID?

1. Any response that gratifies the flesh or exalts anyone other than Jesus Christ.

2. Any response that attracts attention to one's self or causes disruption or distracts other worshippers.

3. Any response that is not characteristically human. For example, animal noises or behavior as a purported means of expressing praise to God would not be in order. Remember: *"God is not the author of confusion"* and *"all things are to be done decently and in order"* (1 Corinthians 14:33,40).

4. Any response that replicates or could be mistaken as typical of the godless behavior of an unregenerate culture (i.e., rock concerts).

5. Any response that overshadows or conflicts with the place of the Word of God in worship. (There are times

87

when the Spirit mov
However, this is not

6. Any response that d
the highest place of
Remember: While G

• WHAT SHOULD I DO?

If you are in a local chu
there is no freedom in the
1. *Pray earnestly for G*
sent revival. Many si
of God's presence. C
experiencing the sam

2. *Continue to worship
times of private dev*
your soul with joy an

3. *Ask the Lord to direc*
enter into spiritual
This must not becon
preacher. <u>Caution:</u> T
as such an attitude is

4. As a last resort and
Spirit, *fellowship with
allows you to be spirit*
there with humility of
leadership.

If you are in a church that
worship and doctrine, often
you may wish to consider th

1. *Prayerfu
tural* and
Rememb
an open
your he
receive t
that—a '
times, it
of doing

2. Along w
*God's Wo
tion? Are
both fait
Word or

3. To whon
be receiv
about so
not to in
an audie
doing. R
against N

4. Ask thes
a. *Are t
b. *Are l
c. *Does

5. Finally,
cannot
fellowsh
honors

There are no simple formulas to follow. God has uniquely created each person. Personalities are different. Experiences vary from extreme to extreme. Consequently, what ministers deeply to one may bypass another. This is the beauty of the family of God. Every member is unique, but all are one in the body of Christ.

How does this fit our topic? The glory of the Lord is surely diminished when our attention is focused on styles of leadership (remember the Corinthians?), hymnbooks versus PowerPoint, or standing/clapping/jumping versus seated/hands raised. The devil is delighted when confusion reigns. He knows that the mission of the Church is being neglected and believers are endangering their own spiritual walk. Yes, the Church needs a revival (renewal) today. To a large degree the burden rests upon those in spiritual leadership and those who have a long history of fellowship with Christ and His church. This is the time to step forward and with maturity offer guidance and stability.

Will you now make a disciplined commitment to pray for a mighty visitation of God in the last days? You can make a difference. Pray that your church will become a fountainhead for genuine revival.

Personal—Family—Church

Community—Nation—World

EMBRACING THE TRUTH

1. The Bible provides insight into God's awesome presence during times of worship. In both Old and New Testaments there is evidence that people *recognized* and *experienced* His powerful presence.

2. In the New Testament, the Holy Spirit was given to empower believers to be witnesses for Christ. Also, the Spirit was manifested in supernatural ways through believers to edify the Church. *There is no scriptural evidence that such manifestations of the Spirit have been discontinued today.*

3. There is a clear scriptural distinction between *manifestations* and **human responses** to the presence of God. One must be careful so the two are not confused. Such responses must be judged in the light of Scripture, with the ultimate purpose of reverencing and ascribing glory to God.

4. The Church must experience **revival** once again. God is ready to fill every hungry heart with His **glory**.

CHAPTER EIGHT

FAITH IS IN A COMA

"Virtues without faith are whitewashed sins.
Unbelief nullifies everything."

Charles Spurgeon

"Without faith, we are as stained glass
windows in the dark."

Anonymous

Faith is foundational to Christian experience. In fact, without it there can be no true relationship with the Almighty.

FAITH IS THE KEY TO SPIRITUAL
LIFE AND VICTORY

Based on the Word of God	Romans 10:17
Basis for salvation experience	Romans 5:1
Basis for man's relationship with God	Hebrews 11:6
Provides link to spiritual reality	Hebrews 11:1
Provides defense against the enemy	Ephesians 6:16
Essential in prayer	James 1:5-6
Prerequisite for the supernatural	Mark 16:17

Marcia and I sat in the doctor's office. Once again he had scolded her for straying from a bland diet. Her ulcer had begun to hemorrhage again.

"Doctor," she asked, "how long will I have to stay on a diet like this?" I will never forget his answer.

He wore dark horn rimmed glasses that were perched halfway down on his nose. He raised his eyebrows and peered over the top of his glasses without changing his expression. "Young lady, you decide how long you want to live." With that, he pushed himself away from his desk and walked out, leaving us to let his verdict sink in.

In those early days of ministry we were traveling as evangelists and often had to stay in homes of pastors or members of the congregation. (Back then revival meetings were 10 days to 2 weeks minimum.) For more than a year we had been earnestly praying for healing. Every night in the services there was a special time of prayer for Marcia's healing. One day she picked up a book in the pastor's home titled, *Now, Therefore Give Me This Mountain*. (I understand it had long been out of print.) It was an incredible story of a young woman who overcame what appeared to be insurmountable obstacles in her life as a foreign missionary. Marcia's faith was at peak level. On the way to church that night, she said, "I believe the Lord will heal me tonight."

We arrived early and prayed. It was simple. There were no special indications that this occasion was any different than the scores of times we had prayed over the past months. However, she said she would like to have a hamburger after church—something that she had been unable to eat for almost 2 years. (I was concerned. We could be up all night after a hamburger, if she were not healed.) Praise the Lord, there were no problems. She slept soundly the entire night. The next day some women from the congregation brought a *hot* (with peppers) Mexican meal for lunch. Marcia ate all the Mexican food she wanted—with no ill effects. From that day to this she has been able to eat anything she desires. (By the way, Mexican food is still her favorite. The hotter the better!)

I do not understand all the ramifications of divine healing. Some are healed and others are not. From many experiences it can be verified that faith alone is not always the determining factor. Some saints—even some who have been used in the gift of healings—have suffered painfully for years. God alone knows the end from the beginning. The plan of God for each individual transcends human reason. In the final analysis, trust is the expression of faith that looks beyond the desired result and clings resolutely to the hand of God.

God's OMNIPOTENCE requires *faith*
God's OMNISCIENCE requires *trust*

Spiritual maturity requires both
faith and *trust*

Divine healing is but one component of this complex subject. Let's turn our attention to the foundational aspects of faith.

• FAITH IS A PREREQUISITE TO EVERYTHING THAT RELATES TO SPIRITUAL LIFE

1. You have to believe that the Bible is the inspired Word of God. There is no where to go until you do. If His Word has no authority to present Christ as man's redeemer, then the whole story is nothing more than ancient fictional literature.

2. You have to believe that Jesus Christ paid the penalty for sin—yours, mine, and every descendant of Adam—by His substitutionary death on the cross. If Jesus is not worthy to be at the Father's right hand, then the whole human race is destined to eternal separation from Almighty God. This concept that was the distinctive of the Early Church.

3. You have to believe that the present-day power of God is greater than all human political systems or even the power of Satan. If human circumstance cannot be altered or overruled by divine intervention (as many have erroneously concluded), we are trapped in a spiral of despair without a future.

"Ask and it will be given to you; seek and ye will find; knock and the door will be opened unto you: For everyone who asks receives; and he who seeks finds; and to him who knocks, the door will be opened" (Matthew 7:7,8, NIV, emphasis mine).

Remember Jesus spoke these words in teaching the multitudes (Sermon on the Mount). Consequently, it bears the same weight as the Beatitudes (Matthew 5) or the Lord's Prayer (Matthew 6) or the admonition to *"seek first the kingdom of God"* (Matthew 6).

In His final discourse with the disciples before going to the cross, Jesus reminded them of their <u>privilege</u> and His <u>promise</u> (John 12-16). *"And I will do whatever you ask in my name, so that the son may bring glory to the Father. You may ask for anything in my name, and I will do it"* (John 14:13,14, NIV). *"If you remain in me and my words remain in you, ask whatever you wish, and it will be given you."* (John 15:7, NIV). *"Until now you have not asked for anything in my name. Ask and you will receive, and your joy will be complete"* (John 16:24, NIV).

The word *faith* is used only twice in the Old Testament, but approximately 250 in the New Testament. Almost 40 of those references are in the book of Romans; while more than 30 are found in Hebrews. In fact, every book in the New Testament, except the Gospel of John and 2 and 3 John, employs the word *faith*. Obviously, John the Beloved understood the importance of faith as noted by the references to the words of Chirst in his Gospel.

If this were such a prevalent theme of New Testament Christianity, then it is imperative that believers today not relegate this basic truth to only a dogma of the church, ignored, or, even worse, discounted as being irrelevant for this generation. How could this happen? The neglect of any scriptural truth, does not suddenly occur. Gradually, ever so slowly, attitudes develop that lead to a low level of faith.

• TOO ENLIGHTENED TO BELIEVE

It seems that one of Satan's loudest arguments against faith is, "You are too intelligent to believe this." From <u>Creation</u> to the <u>virgin birth</u> to the <u>resurrection</u>, human intellect recoils at the idea. "Prove it to me," shouts the skeptic. Of course, it is impossible to intellectually prove the existence of God or His transcendent ways.

Even more troubling are those who sit in the pew and accept only those things that make sense to them. Their religion comes from concluding that following certain biblical principles are personally beneficial. In other words, "This is a good deal for me. After considering all the options this one works the best," they say.

The book of James is often used as a cover for such logic. *"In the same way, faith by itself, if not accompanied by actions is dead. But someone will say, 'You have faith; I have deeds.' Show me your faith without deeds, and I will show you my faith by what I do"* (James 2:17,18, NIV). This is not a dissertation on salvation by works. He is making a strong case for the opposite view. James says unless your your behavior is different, and your relationships are altered, then there is no tangible evidence that you have faith.

This group also has problems with the supernatural intervention of God in human circumstance. To them, divine healing is beyond the pale of reason. Such things happened before the advance of medical technology available today. Who could believe for miraculous deliverance from some life- controlling habit? In a financial crisis the only sensible solution is to borrow money or find another job. (After all, the person is probably to blame for his or her misfortune.) Restoration of family relationships? That's the job for the professional counselor.

Do not misunderstand. In many cases effective solutions can be found. And, we should do our best to avoid plunging into a devastating crisis of our own making. That all sounds so sterile, so tidy and clean. Most of us have learned that life seldom fits into neat packages tied up with pretty ribbons. You may be walking in the sunshine today, but someday it will rain. No matter how intellectually, emotionally or physically strong you are, at some point there will come an intruder who has the ability to overpower you. Don't wait until then to sharpen your faith. We all need God—desperately.

• TOO BEWILDERED TO BELIEVE

The disciples provide a graphic illustration of those who were s confused and bewildered by circumstances. In fact, three of the four Gospel writers make reference to their "doubt" following the resurrection (only John does not). Perhaps Mark's words are the most pungent. *"When they (disciples) heard that Jesus was alive and that she* (Mary Magdalene) *had seen Him, they did not believe it…These* (two walking in the country) *returned and reported it to the rest; but they did not believe them either…Later Jesus appeared to the Eleven as they were eating; he rebuked them for their lack of faith and their stubborn refusal to believe those who had seen him after he had risen"* (Mark 16:11,13,14, NIV).

I tend to cut these disciples a little slack. My reaction could easily have been the same as theirs. They could only see the immediate. Remember, they were still struggling with this whole issue of Roman oppression.   Their concept of Messiah had more to do with the here-and-now than with the unknown future.

Earlier, I related the story of the miraculous (instantaneous) healing of my wife Marcia. But I must also tell you we had one child, Mischelle, and when she was almost 11 she died with a rare form of leukemia. Missy suffered for almost 16 months before the Lord promoted her into His presence. The inevitable question comes. Why? Why would God heal one and not another? Remember, death is the ultimate victory for the child of God. So our comments relate to earthly healing and life. Honesty demands that we simply say we do not have answers for such experiences.   While the pain and grief of that or similar circumstances cannot be described, it would an travesty to doubt the love of our Heavenly Father. God is sovereign. He alone knows past, present, and future.

He does not have to go back to the drawing board with your life. Plan A is not being replaced by Plan B because some event you did not anticipate exploded in your life.

You've got to admire Shadrach, Meshach, and Abednego. King Nebuchadnezzar was furious. They had not bowed to his 90 feet tall image and resolutely told him they had no intention of doing so. But this was not rebellion; this was a spiritual principle. It took an uncompromising commitment to God for these captives to stand up to the leader of the world's greatest empire. Their comments describe a model of faith in action.

"O Nebuchadnezzar, we do not need to defend ourselves before you. If we are thrown into the blazing furnace, the God whom we serve is able to save us. He will rescue us from your power, Your Majesty. But even if he does not, Your Majesty can be sure that we will never serve your gods or worship the gold statue you have set up" (Daniel 3:16-18, NLT). God can—but even if He does not. With exuberance, we tell and retell that story.

Dear saint, weary in the battle, hold on. The Psalmist said it so beautifully, *"Weeping may endure for a night, but joy comes in the morning"* (Psalm 30:5). Let's pause a moment right now and pray earnestly, **"Lord, I believe; help thou my unbelief"** (Mark 9:24).

GOD WILL ALWAYS DO ONE OF TWO THINGS IN TIMES OF CRISIS

He will *deliver out of* the circumstance
or
He will *provide grace to go through* the circumstance

• TOO CONTENTED TO BELIEVE

Nations in the Western world have enjoyed unparalleled prosperity and wealth over the past few decades. One would naturally assume that those so blessed would be among the most grateful. However, this has not been the case. The spiritual devastation is staggering. It boils down in the minds of many to not needing God. Their lifestyle speaks very loudly. There is little doubt that the abundant material blessings from the hand of a benevolent God have become a spiritual detriment to many believers.

The sobering precedent for this faith-choking trap harks all the way back to ancient Israel as they left Egyptian bondage. Talk about looting. The Egyptians were so glad to get rid of them they emptied their safety deposit boxes, as well as their pockets. That night the Israelites walked out with gold, silver, and all the precious jewels and treasures they could carry. But they lost perspective. In only a few days the gold was melted and formed into a golden calf for them to worship as the god who had delivered them from captivity. Sin of the worst kind followed. God was angry enough to destroy the whole crowd. (Read the complete story in Exodus 32.)

The outstanding young man who came to Jesus (Mark 10 says Jesus loved him) asked how to inherit eternal life. He had kept all the commandments. Yet, when the Lord challenged him to sell his possessions and give to the poor, he went away sorrowful (Matthew 19:16-22). In the Parable of the Sower and Seed (Matthew 13; Mark 4; Luke 8), some seed fell among thorns that choked the young plants. Jesus explained to His disciples, *"The thorny ground represents those who hear and accept the Good News, but all too quickly the message is crowded out by the cares of this life, the lure of wealth, and the desire for nice things, so that no crop is produced"* (Mark 4:18,19, NLT, emphasis mine). The infant New Testament Church was only a few weeks old when Ananias and Sapphira got caught in the money-is-more-important-than-faith trap. It cost them their lives—literally (Acts 5:1-11).

Paul's admonition to Timothy is compelling. *"Yet true religion with contentment is great wealth. After all, we didn't bring anything with us when we came into the world and we certainly cannot carry anything with us when we die. So if we have enough food and clothing, let us be content. But people who long to be rich fall into temptation and are trapped by many foolish and harmful desires that plunge them into ruin and destruction. For the love of money is the root of all kinds of evil. And some people, craving money, <u>have wandered from the faith</u> and pierced themselves with many sorrows."* (1 Timothy 6:6-10, NLT, emphasis mine). *"Tell those who are rich in this world not to be proud and <u>not to trust in their money</u>, which will soon be gone. But their trust should be in the living God, who richly gives us all we need for our enjoyment. Tell them to use their money to do good..."* (1 Timothy 6:17,18, emphasis mine).

**If we have God in all things
while they are ours,
We shall have all things in God
when they are taken away.**

Anonymous

Dear brother or sister, so blessed by God in your business, never cease to give Him all the glory. Never turn your eyes from the ***Blessor*** to the ***blessing***. Never allow the **temporary** to blur your vision of the **eternal**. Never, never trade what you can **hold in your hand** for a fleeting moment for what you **hold in your heart**.

• TOO WOUNDED TO BELIEVE

I've heard it scores of times. "But, Pastor, you just don't understand what he/she/they did to me. I don't know if I can ever come back to church again. What did I do to deserve this?"

Reality check. Life is not always fair. People are not perfect, even the most mature among us. Sometimes we are misjudged when our motivation is as pure as pure can be. But, the enemy is not God. We do not run away from Him to find a solution to such injustice. It is in His tender care (and only there) that we can find solace and security.

John the Baptist was in prison. Review his credentials. He was the forerunner of Jesus Christ. John baptized Jesus in the river of Jordan at the very beginning of our Lord's public ministry. He claimed nothing for himself, rather announced boldly that *"He (Christ) must increase, but I must decrease"* (John 3:30). Yet, facing certain death for preaching an uncompromising message, John sends his own disciples to pointedly ask Christ, *"Are you really the Messiah we've been waiting for, or should we keep looking for someone else?"* (Matthew 11:3, NLT). The Lord sent those disciples back with this assurance, *"Go back to John and tell him about what you have heard and seen"* (Matthew 11:4, NLT).

Are you nursing some hurt of the past with around-the-clock care? Secretly, if not openly, are you blaming God for allowing this? Culture says, "Defend yourself. Demand your rights. Don't let him/her get away with treating you like that." Such a cancer of the spirit is deadly to your faith. Faith is stymied by self-pity. The result is weak, fearful

Christians who are barely clinging to spiritual life. The "medical journal" (Word of God) prescribes surgery to restore you to health: *"forgiving one another, even as God for Christ's sake has forgiven you"* (Ephesians 4:32). It may the painful, but the cure is guaranteed. *"We are more than conquerors through him that loved us"* (Romans 8:37).

Perhaps you are still wondering about your own level of faith. Faith is developed by exercise. David faced the *lion* and *bear* before he met *Goliath*. Start where you are. Believe that God will honor His Word. Don't add all the "ifs" and "buts" to your prayer. Forget about back doors. Simply take God's Word at face value. You will be surprised at how quickly you will grow in faith. The church today is facing enormous challenges from culture, both <u>without</u> and <u>within</u>. Only men and women of faith will stand the test.

Keep the faith—Jesus is coming soon!

EMBRACING THE TRUTH

1. Faith is foundational to every aspect of spiritual life. There can be no relationship with God unless it **begins** and is **sustained** by faith.

2. The **development of faith is a process**. The more it is exercised, the stronger it becomes. Life will be filled with tests, all of which have been allowed by God, for the purpose of strengthening the believer's faith.

3. Miraculous intervention in real-life situations still occurs today. While one cannot make demands of God, it is imperative to believe that God **can** and **will** do the humanly impossible when we pray and believe.

4. God is **sovereign**. The believer who explicitly *trusts* Him during times of crisis is exercising a high level of faith. Accepting God's **timing** is vital to a life of faith.

5. The church faces many **temptations** to adopt the cultural standard of **self-sufficiency**. However, the church cannot survive by man's abilities or initiatives. Christ is the Head and the body has no life in itself.

6. Believe for the impossible. God is *omnipotent*. Always be certain that your requests are for **His glory alone** and not for self-gratification.

7. Be willing to hold tenaciously to your faith, even if it means facing strong persecution. It will be worth it all when we see Jesus.

CHAPTER NINE

GRACE IS FREE, NOT CHEAP!

"It is a great deal better to live a holy life than to talk about it. Lighthouses do not ring bells and fire cannons to call attention to their shining—they just shine."

Dwight L. Moody

"Marvelous grace of our loving Lord,
Grace that exceeds our sin and our guilt,
Yonder on Calvary's mount outpoured,
There where the blood of the Lamb was spilt.
Grace, grace, God's grace,
Grace that will pardon and cleanse within;
Grace, grace, God's grace,
grace that is greater than all our sin."

This great hymn, written in the early years of the 20th century, resonates the heartfelt emotion of every born-again believer. To contemplate the grace of God leaves us speechless. Trying to give adequate definition to His grace is impossible.

John Newton (1725-1807) penned what has undoubtedly become the best known of all gospel songs.
"Amazing grace! How sweet the sound,
that saved a wretch like me!
I once was lost, but now am found, was blind,
but now I see."

Mercy and **grace** are important scriptural truths. The word *mercy* is used more than 350 times in the Bible; *grace* is noted approximately 170 times. Mercy is decidedly an Old Testament concept (280 references); grace, a New Testament

The book of James is often used as a cover for such logic. *"In the same way, faith by itself, if not accompanied by actions is dead. But someone will say, 'You have faith; I have deeds.' Show me your faith without deeds, and I will show you my faith by what I do"* (James 2:17,18, NIV). This is not a dissertation on salvation by works. He is making a strong case for the opposite view. James says unless your your behavior is different, and your relationships are altered, then there is no tangible evidence that you have faith.

This group also has problems with the supernatural intervention of God in human circumstance. To them, divine healing is beyond the pale of reason. Such things happened before the advance of medical technology available today. Who could believe for miraculous deliverance from some life- controlling habit? In a financial crisis the only sensible solution is to borrow money or find another job. (After all, the person is probably to blame for his or her misfortune.) Restoration of family relationships? That's the job for the professional counselor.

Do not misunderstand. In many cases effective solutions can be found. And, we should do our best to avoid plunging into a devastating crisis of our own making. That all sounds so sterile, so tidy and clean. Most of us have learned that life seldom fits into neat packages tied up with pretty ribbons. You may be walking in the sunshine today, but someday it will rain. No matter how intellectually, emotionally or physically strong you are, at some point there will come an intruder who has the ability to overpower you. Don't wait until then to sharpen your faith. We all need God—desperately.

The word *faith* is used only twice in the Old Testament, but approximately 250 in the New Testament. Almost 40 of those references are in the book of Romans; while more than 30 are found in Hebrews. In fact, every book in the New Testament, except the Gospel of John and 2 and 3 John, employs the word *faith*. Obviously, John the Beloved understood the importance of faith as noted by the references to the words of Chirst in his Gospel.

If this were such a prevalent theme of New Testament Christianity, then it is imperative that believers today not relegate this basic truth to only a dogma of the church, ignored, or, even worse, discounted as being irrelevant for this generation. How could this happen? The neglect of any scriptural truth, does not suddenly occur. Gradually, ever so slowly, attitudes develop that lead to a low level of faith.

• TOO ENLIGHTENED TO BELIEVE

It seems that one of Satan's loudest arguments against faith is, "You are too intelligent to believe this." From <u>Creation</u> to the <u>virgin birth</u> to the <u>resurrection</u>, human intellect recoils at the idea. "Prove it to me," shouts the skeptic. Of course, it is impossible to intellectually prove the existence of God or His transcendent ways.

Even more troubling are those who sit in the pew and accept only those things that make sense to them. Their religion comes from concluding that following certain biblical principles are personally beneficial. In other words, "This is a good deal for me. After considering all the options this one works the best," they say.

message (130 references). However, they are inextricably joined together. Grace is the divine completion of what mercy began.

Another great old song says, *"Mercy there was great and grace was free, pardon there was multiplied to me. There my burdened soul found liberty, at Calvary."*

Mercy is God not giving us what we deserve; Grace is God giving us what we could never deserve.

Scripture is clear and easily understood on this subject. *"But because of His great love for us, God, who is rich in <u>mercy</u>, made us alive with Christ even when we were dead in transgressions—it is by <u>grace</u> you have been saved. . .For it is by <u>grace</u> you have been save, through faith—and this is not from yourselves, it is the gift of God—not by works, so that no man can boast"* (Ephesians 2:4,5; 8,9, NIV, emphasis mine).

"But when the kindness and love of God our Savior appeared, He saved us, not because of righteous things we have done, but because of His <u>mercy</u>. . .so that, having been justified by his <u>grace</u>, we might become heirs having the hope of eternal life" (Titus 2:4-7, NIV, emphasis mine).

The writer of Hebrews, in the magnificent appeal for Jewish believers to recognize the exalted position of Christ, identifies the throne of God as the *"throne of grace."* After stating that Jesus is our High Priest who understands and sympathizes with our weaknesses, having himself faced temptation but did not sin, the believer is encouraged to come before this heavenly throne. *"Let us then approach the <u>throne of grace</u> with confidence, so that we may receive <u>mercy</u> and find <u>grace</u> to help us in our time of need"* (Hebrews 4:14-16, NIV, emphasis mine).

Notice the opening greetings in Paul's letters. The salutation in 11 epistles includes the expression, *"Grace and peace from God."* In his letters to Timothy he expanded it by saying, *"Grace, mercy, and peace from God"* (emphasis mine). His mercy and grace always bring peace.

Yet, as incomprehensible as God's grace is, it can still be abused by those who attempt to use it as a free pass to excuse sin and/or its dastardly consequences. Has the church overreacted to the despair of this generation? In the sincere desire to reach those whose lives have been devastated, is it possible that the balanced message of grace and judgment has been virtually omitted? Or, even worse, has the cultural climate of tolerance and acceptance (i.e., homosexual lifestyle) crept into the house of God? Is there any such thing as sin today or have we gently explained it away? The Scripture says, *"For the time has come that judgment must begin at the house of God: and if it first begin at us, what shall be the end of them that obey not the gospel of God? And, if the righteous scarcely be saved, where shall the ungodly and the sinner appear?"* (1 Peter 4:17,18). Peter is calling the Early Church to a life of *"holiness,"* which was commanded by God who himself is holy.

• What do you mean by unconditional?

Those who reject salvation as being possible only through Jesus Christ make statements like, "God is too good to send anyone to hell." Incidentally, that is true. If anyone is eternally separated from God, it will be because that person chose to reject Him, not that God had some vendetta against her/him. Such thinking is rooted in an erroneous concept of man's salvation or lostness. Believers understand that our goodness or badness does not qualify nor disqualify us to be saved. Because we are descendants of Adam, fellowship with God has been severed. This holy God can accept us back into a restored relationship only *in* and *through* the sacrifice of His Son. This is grace, pure and simple.

Such foolish thinking might be expected from the spiritually blind. But there are also those who profess Christ whose understanding of grace is skewed. Did you ever hear a believer say, "I know this is wrong, but God's love is unconditional"? Such a comment begs the question: "What do you mean by *unconditional?*" To many, it simply means *no matter what.* Is there a scriptural definition of God's love? Let's attempt to discover the biblical response.

1. <u>Yes</u>, His love is unconditional if one means that it is *impossible to earn or deserve it by good deeds or works.* This is, in fundamental nature, the rationale for grace.

2. <u>Yes</u>, His love is unconditional if one means that it is *made available at His initiative and unilaterally.* That is, God's love did not come through a negotiated contract. According to Paul's letter to the Romans, *"God demonstrates His own love for us in this: while we were still sinners, Christ died for us"* (Romans 5:8, NIV).

3. <u>Yes</u>, His love is unconditional if one means that it is *extended to the sinner for the purpose of bringing him/her to repentance and restoration of fellowship with God.* Even in warning of the coming judgment, the apostle Peter reminds the church that God is *"long suffering to us-ward, not willing that any should perish, but that all should come to repentance"* (2 Peter 3:9).

4. <u>NO</u>, His love is not unconditional if one means that it is *man's license to excuse sin and live in rebellion against God.* In making this point, Paul was emphatic. *"What shall we*

say, then? *Shall we go on sinning so that grace may increase? By no means!"* (Romans 6:1,2, NIV). "God forbid!" is the wording in the KJV.

5. <u>NO</u>, His love is not unconditional if one means that *God will never punish wrongdoing or will always prevent the consequences of sinful behavior.* Thankfully, none of us are sitting on the bench in the courtroom. God alone knows all the facts. He is the only one who can see the entire picture.

6. <u>NO</u>, His love is not unconditional if one means that *ultimately, in eternity, everyone will be rescued from punishment for their sin and rebellion against God while here on earth.* Between grace and judgment is the line called *justice.* At the eternal day, His very nature will require that justice prevail.

• At my convenience or for His glory?

A member of the worship team was discovered to be living an immoral lifestyle and was asked to step down from this responsibility. Frustrated that he would have to give up his ministry, he countered the spiritual authority by saying, "God has forgiven me; why can't you?" What's wrong with that picture? God's grace was being used only as a means to an end— to secure what the individual wanted.

Those who have been delivered from life-controlling habits, and what is commonly described as the "depths of sin," will find ample reason to rejoice in the personal application of grace. Regardless of how bad or good we were before coming to Jesus, we have been made over from the inside out. Those who disciple people who have been addicted to drugs or alcohol or involved in other behavior not accepted in society, repeatedly emphasize that they must be certain that accepting Christ to this individual is more than a means to avoid incarceration or some other form of societal punishment. One could sympathize with a frightened youngster for not wanting to be placed in a prison with hardened criminals. Yet the grace of God is so much more than a convenient way to avoid personal accountability or inconvenience for our actions.

Let's shift our focus from those who are struggling with mammoth issues, to those who have been in the church for an extended time. Perhaps by comparing two Old Testament kings, **Saul** and **David**, the significance of this truth can be captured. Both of these kings of Israel (first and second, and two of only three who served the entire nation) sinned against Jehovah God. In both situations they were confronted by the prophet of God. The response was identical. Each said, *"I have sinned."* Here, however, the similarities end. Saul was rejected as monarch and the kingdom was not even given to one of his descendants. On the other hand, Jesus Christ, the eternal King, was a direct descendant of King David. How can one account for this? Did God play favorites?

Saul was given as assignment from God through the prophet Samuel. *"Now go, attack the Amalekites and totally destroy everything that belongs to them. Do not spare them; put to death men and women, children and infants, cattle and sheep, camels and donkeys"* (1 Samuel 15:3, NIV). Many will recall the outcome of this engagement of war. Saul *"and the army spared Agag and the best of the sheep and cattle, the fat calves and lambs—everything that was good"* (1 Samuel 15:9, NIV). When the Lord revealed this to Samuel, he approached King Saul about the battle. Proudly, Saul said that the mission had been accomplished. When Samuel pushed for further details about the animals, the king maintained his innocence: *"I did obey the Lord."* Notice, he blamed the soldiers for bringing back the animals, but justified them in that there actions were for the purpose of sacrifice. When finally he acknowledged wrongdoing, he still tried to exonerate himself. *"I have sinned. I violated the Lord's command and your instructions. I was afraid of the people and so I gave in to them"* (1 Samuel 15:24, NIV). He only sought for mercy and grace to protect his own skin. God (nor Samuel) was buying any of it. At this moment, the old prophet advised Saul, *"The Lord has torn the Kingdom of Israel from you today"* (1 Samuel 15:27, NIV).

David—foolish David. Caught in a trap of fleshly lust, he committed adultery and murder. Pretty bad stuff, don't you think? God sent Nathan the prophet to point a finger in the king's self-righteous face and declare, *"You are the man"* (2 Samuel 12:7, NIV). David's response? *"I have sinned against the Lord"* (2 Samuel 12:13, NIV). No excuses, no trying to justify himself—just an honest admission of sin. One only has to read **Psalm 51** to hear the broken heart of David. He pled for God's forgiveness and the restoration of His presence in his life. A loving God accepted David's sincerity. To this day believers refer to David as *"a man after God's own heart"* (1 Samuel 13:14).

God is not passing out grace like toys at Christmas. That marvelous grace, though surely for our benefit, is for His glory. The children of God are *"his glorious inheritance"* which is *"in accordance with his pleasure and will—to the praise of His glorious grace"* (Ephesians 1:7, NIV). Every redeemed child of God is by any standard of measurement a trophy of grace.

• Did you really repent?

Here is the scenario. The believer knows that a certain act is unscriptural—sinful, in a word. Yet, he rationalizes that after the sin has been committed, he will repent and ask the Lord for forgiveness. Once the person got what he wanted, all the while aware of God's disapproval, he would then say he is sorry for disobeying. Can we presume upon the grace of God in such a manner? Did the person really repent? Simply saying, "I'm sorry" does not necessarily constitute true repentance. Here, in my opinion, is a major problem that has invaded the church today. The shrug of the shoulders at sin—a cavalier attitude toward God's grace—is alarming.

In recent years pollsters have repeatedly concluded there is little, if any, difference in the behavior of those who profess to be born again and those who make no such claim. The grace of God is not an indulgence, nor is it a therapeutic rationalization for sinful behavior. *God is in the business of forgiving sin—not excusing it.*

To the woman caught in an adulterous act, Jesus extended grace. (Did you ever wonder where the man was? He was guilty of the same sin.) When her accusers suddenly developed guilty consciences, the Lord said, *"Neither do I condemn you."* He then solemnized her responsibility by adding, *"Go now and leave your life of sin"* (John 8:11, NIV). Never once do we hear even a hint from the Lord that so long as we keep coming to Him it is not necessary to completely abandon our sin. This is not extreme. Many new converts have unscriptural habits deeply imbedded into the fabric of their lives. Who among us would presume to measure the grace of God that He will extend to such tender ones? Still His plan is plain and simple—leave your sin.

In his letters to the Ephesian and Colossian saints, the apostle Paul urges them to *"put off the old man"* and *"put on the new man"* (Ephesians 4:22-24; Colossians 3:9,10). The New Living Translation powerfully expresses the Ephesians passage. *"Since you have heard all about Him and have learned the truth that is in Jesus, throw off your old evil nature and your former way of life, which is rotten through and through, full of lust and deception. Instead, there must be a spiritual renewal of your thoughts and attitudes. You must display a new nature because you are a new person, created in God's likeness—righteous, holy, and true."*

> God's grace will forgive our past sins and help us to overcome present ones, but His grace will never make us *comfortable* in or *comfortable* about them.

• Abundant grace is carefully measured

The Children of Israel were given specific instructions concerning the daily supply of *manna* (Exodus 16:10-30) during their 40 years in the wilderness. Each day they were to collect only as much as was required for each member of the family. If they gathered more than the stipulated amount, by the next morning it was full of worms. (On the sixth day they were to collect twice the normal amount, as there was no manna on the Sabbath.) This is a noteworthy lesson about the grace of God. Each day's supply is fresh for that day. It cannot be stored as only the needed amount is provided. Yet, there is never any lack.

Suffering with a *"thorn in the flesh"* Paul sought the Lord for deliverance. None came. Instead, he discovered the abundance of grace in time of trial. The Lord's words were reassuring. *"My grace is sufficient for you, for my power is made perfect in weakness"* (2 Corinthians 12:9, NIV).

Have you ever said, "I could never go through that"? Marcia did. When a 6 year old friend of our daughter Mischelle died with cystic fibrosis, Marcia wept for her parents but said she could never handle such a loss. Not many months after that very day, we were staring in the face of death in our own little family. Mischelle, our only child, went to be with the Lord at age 10. It was a devastating experience. There were some very difficult days. (For all who have gone through the death of a family member, you know that you never get over it.) Over the ensuing years, by the grace of God, Marcia has been able to share a dynamic testimony of daily grace that has given strength and hope to thousands of women (and men) in the clutches of situations that defy any reasonable solutions.

God's grace is like an old-fashioned balance scale.
When the pressures of life begin to overbalance our lives,
He adds enough grace to keep us from being overwhelmed.
The supply is always abundantly adequate for every circumstance.

• God's grace is for living as well as dying

When we arrive in heaven, it will be the ultimate expression of divine grace. On the other hand, grace is also for the present—the here and now. Have you ever wondered how unbelievers face the crisis moments? In the same breath you thanked God for His *sustaining grace*. Yet, over and over again, believers express bewilderment and confusion at the vicissitudes of daily life. It somehow escapes them that salvation does not extricate any of us from the daily associations with a depraved society.

Late one evening while driving home from a speaking engagement, I heard a well-known radio/TV preacher observe, "If Paul had had any faith, he would have never been in prison." I have no clue how or where he found that in scripture. (I immediately switched the radio dial.) To assume that believers are exempted from the *trials of life* by the exercise of faith is unscriptural. No child of God need ever be <u>defeated</u> or <u>destroyed</u> by circumstances, but that is totally different than demanding that God do it our way. As discussed previously, faith is essential to every aspect of our relationship with God. However, it is not free standing in the sense that all I must do to alter any event or circumstance of life is to have a proper degree of faith. So, why do we encounter mountain-sized difficulties—the kind that can only be overcome by a special portion of God's grace?

1. <u>The whole creation is still under the curse.</u> *Death has been defeated, but it has not yet been destroyed.* According to the Resurrection chapter in 1 Corinthians, the apostle declares that the *"last enemy to be destroyed is death"* (1 Corinthians 15:26).

2. <u>Satan has been allowed certain liberties on this earth for a period of time.</u> Jesus described Satan as the *"prince of this world"* three times in His final teaching session with the disciples before He went to the cross (John 12:31; 14:30; 16:11)? Paul named him as the *"god of this world"* (2 Corinthians 4:4) and *"the prince of the power of the air"* (Ephesians 2:2).

3. <u>Sin has consequences.</u> If you accept the premise of Scripture, you cannot escape the law of *"sowing and reaping."* On one occasion I led a woman to the Lord who had been openly living an adulterous life. In the small community where she lived and worked, it was well known. After a few weeks of her newfound joy of sins forgiven, she sat in my office with tears. "Why won't people forget?" she sobbed. "I thought God forgave me."

Gently, I explained that God had indeed washed her sins away, but that people are often skeptical and it will be the evidence of a changed life that will convince them of her experience in Christ. Sometimes the web of past sin is too tangled to ever be resolved. Never again can that portion of life be returned to its original place. Here is where the grace of God can so *wonderfully* and *wondrously* be appropriated.

> While God's grace freely forgives our sins, it does not necessarily follow that His grace eradicates all the consequences of wrongdoing.

    4. <u>God tests His own children.</u> This is the part we don't like. Brother Job had it made. Everything one could desire—family, friends, wealth, prestige—was at his disposal. He was a devout man who loved God and hated evil. God recognized it, and so did the devil. At the accusation of Satan that Job's motivation was selfish, God <u>allowed</u> Satan (on two occasions) to take his best shot at Job. Although he expressed deep emotions, this godly man did not compromise his faith. The end result was that Job overcame, by the grace of God, and the equivalent of all that had been taken away was restored. Wouldn't it be wonderful if God could say to the devil about us, "No matter what happens, he or she will still trust Me"?

    The Book of Hebrews speaks to this issue. In encouraging Jewish believers not to *"cast away your confidence"* (10:35), the author provides a powerful record of faith in Hebrews 11. After charging them to *"lay aside every weight, and the sin which does so easily beset us"* and to *"run with patience the race that is set before us"* these young believers are admonished to *"look unto Jesus the author and finisher of our faith; who for the joy that was set before him endured the cross, despising the shame, and is set down at the right hand of the throne of God"* (Hebrews 12:1,2). That verse provides ample reason to rejoice. But, listen to what comes next. *"Consider Him who endured such opposition from sinful men, so that you will not grow weary and lose heart"* (12:3, NIV).

Jesus, the Son of God, endured suffering, and it would be wise for us to look carefully at His example so we do not give up our faith. The writer amplifies the message: *"My son, do not make light of the Lord's discipline, and do not lose heart when he rebukes you...endure hardship as discipline; God is treating you as sons"* (Hebrews 12:5-7, NIV). The end product? *"No discipline seems pleasant at the time, but painful. Later on, however, it produces a harvest of righteousness and peace for those who have been trained by it"* (Hebrews 12:11, NIV).

One point to be considered is that **discipline** and **punishment** are not synonymous. As the child of God is growing to spiritual maturity, discipline is required, just as it is for a child in the development of personal and social skills. Nonetheless, grace is needed as we often do not fully comprehend all that God is doing in our lives. What a blessed thought. He loves us enough to prevent spiritual self-destruction and so these tests come with regularity. At the same time, He is supplying the means by which we may endure the test.

The church must clearly articulate this message. Many are confused; others are bone weary from fighting the battle alone; and still others have lost hope and question the love of God. "God's grace will see you through the darkest night in the deepest valley" needs to be an oft repeated refrain from every pulpit. Mature believers who have overcome should frequently testify to the marvel of divine grace. The church must never fall prey to the immediate self-gratification syndrome demanded by contemporary culture. It has been said, "You can pay now and enjoy later or enjoy now and pay later." Either way you will pay. The redeemed saints who are *"looking forward to the city with foundations, whose architect and builder is God"* (Hebrews 11:10, NIV) always choose the former with confident assurance.

EMBRACING THE TRUTH

1. **Mercy** and **grace** are attributes of God expressed toward His fallen creation. By His **mercy** sinful man is not consumed. By His **grace** sinful man can be restored to fellowship with a holy God through Jesus Christ.

2. Grace is not to be taken lightly. It is not a *right*, rather it is a unique privilege for the sincere of heart. Grace is not a personal possession by which God can be manipulated for our own personal gratification.

3. Grace provides forgiveness for sins of every dimension and degree, but it does not necessarily eliminate the earthly consequences of sinful behavior.

4. Grace is for living in the present as well as providing an entrance into the eternal future. *One is not ready to die by grace, until he has learned to live by grace.*

5. Because of His love, God often disciplines His children to conform them to the *"image of Christ"* (Romans 8:29). At the same time, He supplies sufficient grace to experience glorious victory in daily struggles.

CHAPTER TEN

WHO SAYS THERE IS JUST ONE WAY?

*"You can enter God's Kingdom only through
the narrow gate. The highway to hell is
broad, and its gate is wide for many who
choose the easy way. But the gateway to life
is small, and the road is narrow, and only a
few ever find it."*

Jesus (Matthew 7:13,14, NLT)

You can't miss it. That is, if you believe the Bible.
However, unless you accept the Word of God as absolute
truth there is no basis for discussion of the divinely exclusive
plan for man's redemption in and through Jesus Christ. Let
me not get ahead of myself. More about the basis for faith
found in the Word a bit later.

Our culture is asking the question. "How do you know for
certain there is **only one way to eternal life**?" Unfortunately,
many believers cannot give a definitive answer from Scripture
and others waffle when pointedly ask the question. Imagine
the captain of a spaceship not knowing how to read the information provided by the computers onboard or, if he could,
being uncertain as to whether the data was accurate. Not too
many would be willing to risk such a flight.

Is it any wonder many are leaving the organized church
and searching for a spiritual experience from who knows
where? Perhaps of equal concern are those who occupy a
pew week after week without any compulsion to encounter
the living Christ. The Church our Lord established was not
to be filled with spectators who semi-claimed to be His followers. The power of the Spirit was given on the Day of

Pentecost (birthday of the New Testament church), enabling that small group to be so convinced that Jesus Christ was the Son of God that they would stand with holy boldness to declare the message—even to the point of sacrificing their own lives. But let's start long before the earthly visitation of Christ to discover how the true believer can establish the exclusivity of God's redemptive purposes.

• GOD'S PROGRESSIVE REVELATION

1. <u>In the Garden of Eden</u>   (Genesis 1-3, NIV)

"Then God said, 'Let us make man in our own image'...So God created man in His own image" (1:26,27). *"The Lord God took the man and put him in the Garden of Eden to work it and to take care of it. And the Lord God <u>commanded</u> the man, 'You are free to eat from any tree in the garden; but you <u>must not</u> eat from the tree of the knowledge of good and evil, for when you eat of it you <u>will sure-ly die</u>'"* (2:15-17, emphasis mine).

There is little room for doubt. God told Adam that there is only one way. And, it happened just as He said. Adam and Eve died spiritually (later physically) because of their disobedience. The horrible consequences of their behavior have negatively affected the entire human race. Paul articulates that we share culpability with Adam, *"for all have sinned and come short of the glory of God"* (Romans 3:23). Yet, it is that depraved nature, the bent toward evil which emanates from sin in the Garden of Eden, that haunts us all until we come to a personal relationship with Christ.

The very first prophecy concerning Christ is found in Genesis 3:15 when God cursed the serpent. *"And I will put enmity between you and the woman, and between your offspring and hers; he shall crush your head, and you will strike his heel."*

2. <u>Acceptable sacrifices</u> (Genesis 3,4, NIV)

After Adam and Eve sinned *"they sewed fig leaves together and made coverings for themselves"* (3:7). But God chose differently for them. *"The Lord God made garments of skin for Adam and his wife and clothed them"* (3:21). A blood sacrifice was required to atone for their sins. That is extremely important in understanding the revelation of God's redemptive plan.

Look how this played out in the lives of the first two children born to the human race. *"Now Abel kept flocks, and Cain worked the soil. In the course of time Cain brought some of the fruits of the soil as an offering to God. But Abel brought fat portions from some of the firstborn of his flock. The Lord looked with favor on Abel and his offering, but on Cain and his offering He did not look with favor"* (4:2-5). Again, God did not accept an offering from vegetation. There had to be an animal, thus requiring a sacrificial death.

Later, under the Law of Moses, God gave explicit instructions concerning the types of sacrifices He would accept. In the New Testament Book of Hebrews (written to Jewish believers), the writer, in making comparison with and distinction between the Old and New Covenants says, *"Without the shedding of blood there is no forgiveness"* (Hebrews 9:22). All of this was God progressively showing the only way that man could once again enter into His fellowship.

3. The Ten Commandments   (Exodus 20)

This is Almighty God's TOP 10 list. And, No. 1 is: *"Thou shalt have no other gods before me."* *Straightforward, don't you think?"* No. 2 ? *"Thou shalt not make unto thee any graven images...thou shalt not bow down to them. . .for I the Lord thy God am a jealous God."* So far no questions about what He was saying. No. 3 ? *"Thou shalt not take the name of the Lord thy God in vain."* No. 4 ? *"Six days shalt thou labor and do all thy work; but the seventh day is the Sabbath of the Lord thy God...the Lord blessed the Sabbath day and hallowed it."*

Did you ever wonder why these commandments did not begin with *"Thou shalt not kill"* or *"Thou shalt not steal"*? These are outworkings of a proper relationship with God. Man does not begin with man and try to find his way to God. That, in effect, is the fallacy of human philosophy. God simply says He is the only God. His creation is not to speak or act in any way that would not reverence Him as the one true God.

4. Obedience is the basic requirement

In one of his final sermons to the Children of Israel, (Deuteronomy 28) Moses succinctly describes what will happen *"if thou shalt hearken diligently unto the voice of the Lord thy God, to observe and to do all His command-ments."* It is all good. In fact, Moses is so certain of God's approval that he says, *"All these blessings shall come on thee, and overtake thee."* What a promise. You cannot escape the blessings in your home, health, busi-ness, politically, and spiritually.

On the opposite side of the page, with the same degree of certainty and dimension of severity, Moses warns the people of God they will be cursed, if they refuse to obey the commands of the Lord. So simple and elementary. Just obey God. Of course this clashes with man's depraved nature. So, for all our good intentions, it is not possible for any of us to enter into relationship with a holy God by our own efforts. But there is wonderful news.

• JESUS, THE ULTIMATE REVELATION

1. The Son of Man—Son of God question

In the four Gospels, Christ is referred to as the *"Son of man"* more than 80 times. Many of these references are the Lord speaking of himself. Only a few times is He addressed as the *"Son of God"* by the biographical authors. It is significant that the most frequent recognition of His deity came from the devil during a time of temptation in the wilderness or by demon spirits when He confronted them in some individual.

Jesus was fully man while living in an earthly body here on earth. He grew up physically as a normal child. He got hungry, needed sleep (even to the point of sleeping through a storm), and experienced the whole range of human emotion. The writer of Hebrews says: *"This High Priest of ours understands our weaknesses, for he faced all of the same temptations we do, yet he did not sin"* (Hebrews 4:15, NLT).

The 12 disciples were with Jesus constantly for approximately 3 years. Indeed, they saw the miracles and heard His teachings. They also saw His humanity.

Is it any wonder that Christ told Simon Peter that his declaration, *"Thou art the Christ, the Son of the living God"* (Matthew 16:24) did not come by human intellect? The challenge for that generation was to accept Christ as the Messiah. This was especially difficult since their concept was that Messiah would bring immediate deliverance from Roman oppression. Some of the prevalent attitudes of that day were not unlike some today.

ATTITUDES TOWARD GOD'S REVEALED WORD IN THE TIME OF CHRIST

Pharisees	*externalized*
Sadducees	*secularized*
Scribes	*professionalized*
Herodians	*compromised*
Zealots	*politicized*
Temple Traders	*commercialized*
Jewish people	*materialized*
Disciples	*glamorized*

Today, it would be much easier for us to accept Christ as the Son of God. After all, He was crucified and resurrected. He did ascend to His Father's right hand. The Word of God confirms this. Plus, the almost 2,000 year history of the New Testament church should leave no doubt that man's redemption (justification, regeneration, salvation) comes from only one source—Jesus Christ. Yet, for all the evidence, many remain content to add our Lord's name to a list of those teachers who have been widely accepted.

After having ministered in New York City one Friday evening, we were having dinner in one of the popular diners in the area. A young woman who had been in the service had been witnessing to a young Muslim waiter there. She came to our table and asked that I speak with him about Jesus. In a few moments he ventured to our table and initiated a conversation about the distinctions between Islam and Christianity. He quickly stated that Muslims also believed in Jesus—as a prophet. When I countered with the biblical truth that Christ was *more than a prophet*, and as the Son of God He has divine status that is unequalled by Abraham, Moses, or even Mohammed, he insisted I "prove it." We both knew that what He was asking could not be done. So I gently tried to tell him that knowing Christ in personal relationship was not achieved by human intellect but rather by faith in the finished work of the cross. Many still struggle with the Son of Man—Son of God issue.

2. <u>Message at Pentecost</u>

The birthday of the New Testament church. The Day of Pentecost is significant and should be celebrated by believers just as we do the birth and resurrection of Christ. It was to be in the Spirit's power that this small band of disciples was to heed the final instruction of Christ before He ascended. *"But ye shall receive power after that the Holy Ghost is come upon you: and ye shall be witnesses unto Me both in Jerusalem, and in all Judea, and in Samaria, and unto the uttermost part of the earth"* (Acts 1:8). Now, only a few days later, full of the Spirit, Peter (the same one who had denied Christ) stands with boldness to declare the message of salvation through Christ.

While I personally believe in the infilling of the Holy Spirit with the accompanying evidence of *"speaking with other tongues"*, Peter's message at Pentecost was not exclusively concerning the phenomenon the 120 had just received. Listen to what he said in his address to an audience representing nations from all across the then-known world. *"This man was handed over to you by God's set purpose and foreknowledge; and you, with the help of wicked men, put him to death by nailing him to the cross. But God raised him from the dead...God has raised this Jesus to life, and we are all witnesses of the fact...Therefore let all Israel be assured of this: God has made this Jesus, whom you crucified, both Lord and Christ"* (Acts 2:23-36, NIV).

After the healing of the lame man at the temple gate (Acts 3), Peter again emphasizes that Christ was crucified and resurrected. It was *"by faith in the name of Jesus"* that this man had been healed. When pushed by the Sanhedrin for an explanation of this miracle, Peter eiterates, *"If we are being called to account today for an act of kindness shown to a cripple, and are asked how he was healed, then know this: it is by the name of Jesus Christ of Nazareth, whom you crucified but whom God raised from the dead, that this man stands before you healed"* (Acts 4:9,10, NIV). Then comes the zinger. <u>*"Salvation is found in no one else, for there is no other name under heaven given to men by which we must be saved"*</u> (Acts 4:12, NIV, emphasis mine).

One could recount Peter's personal call to follow Christ, His declaration at Caesarea Philippi, and the experience on the Mount of Transfiguration during his discipleship training program. It would prove to be a wealth of evidence as to why he should be believed. Additionally, he had received the infilling of the Holy Spirit, which Christ had repeatedly promised to His disciples (John 13-16). Another obvious confirmation of divine purpose. The apostle recognized that some would still question the validity of such claims. Consequently, in his last letter (2 Peter) he emphasizes his record is not some *"cunningly devised fable"* (1:16-18). Without any reservation he cites the authority of Scripture as verification of his experience (1:19-21).

The further you go, the more convinced you become that God's plan is not some optional, spur-of-the-moment idea that a few radical men and women chose to follow for personal gratification. Step by step, God was manifesting himself among His fallen creation for the express purpose of restoring the broken relationship.

3. The Judaizers wanted to be certain

How do you transition from the *Old* to the *New* covenant? Some of the earliest Jewish believers—often referred to as Judaizers—found the leap too large. Consequently, they insisted that the ceremonial aspects of the Law of Moses be maintained. Specifically, they were concerned about the rite of circumcision. In Acts 15, the council determined that this and other such aspects of the Law were not required for salvation. Repeatedly, the apostle Paul (apostle sent to the Gentiles) emphasizes that circumcision is not a substitute for or even a component of true faith. In his discussion of Abraham as the *"father of faith"* (Romans 4), he nixes the idea of salvation by works. Again, in Galatians he warns against those who *"desire to make a fair show in the flesh, they constrain you to be circumcised"* (6:12). His conclusion? *"God forbid that I should glory, save in the cross of our Lord Jesus Christ, by whom the world is crucified unto me, and I unto the world. For in Christ Jesus neither circumcision availeth anything, nor uncircumcision, but a new creature"* (6:14,15).

Just a word in defense of these early Jewish followers of Christ. This change was huge. They were the only monotheistic people in the world. Others were polytheistic—having numerous gods, and often living evil lives. Wanting to be certain they did not violate any of the commandments of Almighty God, these Jewish believers were struggling with this issue. It parallels what pastors hear today. "Pastor, we need to be careful. We have never done it this way before." But in His wisdom and love, God gave the wonderful Book of Hebrews. The theme of the entire book is to reveal conclusively that Jesus Christ is *better*.

CHRIST AS "BETTER" IN THE BOOK OF HEBREWS

Chapters 1,2	Christ is better than angels
Chapter 3	Christ is better than Moses
Chapter 4	Christ is better than Joshua
Chapter 5	Christ is better than Aaron
Chapter 7	Christ is better than the Levitical priesthood
Chapters 9,10	Christ is better than the sacrificial animals
Chapters 11,12	Christ is better than the Old Testament heroes

---

4. <u>Paul should know</u>

Do you ever paint mental pictures of Bible characters? Here is my image of Paul. Deeply furrowed brow. Bushy eyebrows. Thick, horn-rimmed glasses. Intense to the point of intimidation. Often you hear him speaking of the *"mystery"* (reference Ephesians and Colossians) of Christ and the gospel. I see him slapping his forehead with the palm of his hand, saying over and over, "How could I have missed it?"

But, let's go back for a moment. Saul (later Paul) did not comprehend this mystery, in spite of all his years of study. Remember, he was a renowned teacher of the Law of Moses. He knew the Scriptures very well. But, it was the Damascus road experience (Acts 9)—the *revelation of Christ*—that changed his life. Now he is deeply committed to Christ and to sharing this message with both Jew and Gentile. It is such a driving passion that he considers all of his previous assets as *"rubbish, that I may gain Christ and be found in Him, not having a righteousness of my own that comes from the law, but that which is through faith in Christ—the righteousness that comes from God and is by faith"* (Philippians 3:8,9, NIV).

Could a man of this intelligence and knowledge be duped? Was he just looking for one more new experience? It hardly seems possible, since he was such a zealot for the Mosaic covenant that he was the Ambassador of Persecution to followers of Christ. As an official witness, Saul watched the coats of those who stoned Stephen (Acts 7:58-8:1). It is much easier to believe that the Spirit arrested his heart and revealed that Christ, through death and resurrection, was the one and only atoning provision for man's sin.

• IS THE BIBLE REALLY ABSOLUTE TRUTH?

This is the core question. Is the Bible the inspired *"Word of God"* or is it just one of many good books offering insights into moral values? Notice that all the evidence presented in this chapter is from God's Word. If it is not a reliable source of information, then all that Christians teach and believe is only a matter of personal choice. One of the most serious concerns facing the church today involves scriptural authority. Has our culture saturated our minds with doubts? Can we no longer accept the words of Old and New Testament writers as being inspired—God breathed, penned under the influence of the Holy Spirit? Are men and women, both in the pulpit and the pew, repeating words that deep down within their hearts, they do not believe? Brothers and sisters, it is more than a slippery slope. It is the fast track to spiritual disaster.

The Word is the passageway into faith. Any other message is a non-gospel. *"So then faith cometh by hearing, and hearing by the word of God"* (Romans 10:17). From Genesis to Revelation the message is the redemption of sinful mankind in and through Jesus Christ. Everything else that one does is ancillary. You have to begin with Christ. **He is the One and only way to eternal life.**

EMBRACING THE TRUTH

1. God created man for the specific purpose of enjoying a spiritual relationship (fellowship) with Him. When man (Adam and Eve) sinned in the Garden of Eden, they died spiritually and began the process of physical death.

2. God has progressively revealed himself to man in his fallen state; however, the eternal plan of redemption is fulfilled **only in Christ Jesus**.

3. The scriptural record is *inspired* and both Old and New Testaments present relevant truth for all generations. It is the highest level of authority for both faith and practice for all believers.

4. The *written Word* is illuminated by the Holy Spirit so that Christ is exalted as the *living Word*.

IS BIBLICAL PREACHING FOR THE ARCHIVES?

"The best way to revive a church is to build a fire in the pulpit."

Dwight L. Moody

"I believe that the absence of sound doctrine is another proof that the Church is in need of revival. Sound doctrine has to a great degree ceased. It happened when ministers in the pulpit stopped preaching sound doctrine for fear of how it would be received."

Charles H. Spurgeon

One of America's leading Bible scholars sat in my office after having lectured to Bible and theology professors from four church-related colleges/ universities and three universities from the public (non-church related) sector. His address to these men and women had stressed the correlation between *hermeneutics* and *homiletics*. (Hermeneutics, by definition, being the proper interpretation of Scripture; homiletics, the proper application of Scripture.) I was intrigued that this scholar (author of more than 50 books) had chosen to speak to these other scholars on this particular subject, so, I ventured a question. Why was he so passionate about this matter, which would seem rather basic to the highly degreed persons who had been present?

His answer caught me a bit off guard. He told of a conversation with a well-known pastor who had recently confronted him on his approach to Scripture. "Doctor," the pastor had said, "you are still preaching a linear gospel. This is a sound-byte generation. They don't have the time nor inclination for such preaching."

I responded, "But when these people face a crisis in life, which of the sound-bytes do they choose? Sound-bytes do not reveal the character or ways of God in a manner other than to stir the emotions or provide an incomplete view of His redemptive purposes." He agreed, concluding that his purpose had been to reinforce the absolute necessity of a clear presentation of the gospel of Christ.

But in spite of those who champion the cause for biblical exposition, in many quarters preaching has fallen on hard times. In some thriving congregations, the pulpit has been moved from the center of the platform (if there even is a pulpit). The worship team and their accompanists occupy the "stage" while the pastor and ministerial associates sit on the front row (or elsewhere) in the congregation. Before you conclude that this is the work of one who is tied to tradition, think for a moment as to why the pulpit was located in the center in the platform. It, by its very position, expressed the centrality of God's Word. Growing up in Texas I heard of First Baptist in Dallas all my life. Two pastors served for more than 100 years. What a record. How did this happen? They focused on preaching God's Word.

Often being a guest speaker in local churches, I can attest that there has been a major shift in emphasis from *preaching* to *celebration* in recent years. There are numerous anecdotes that could be related here. Suffer one or two vignettes to emphasize this significant point.

Recently we were in a church that did not even have a pulpit. The pastor never even went onto the platform during the entire service. When I preached that day, I stood in front of the communion table and borrowed a music stand from the platform for my Bible and notes. Actually, there was no room on the platform for a pulpit.

On another occasion, the morning worship started at 10 a.m. and the pastor introduced me to preach at 11:45 a.m. He apologized to the congregation as he knew some could not remain past the noon hour for Communion. Imagine the level of interest they had in hearing a sermon at that point.

One final illustration. As we gathered for prayer in the pastor's office, all the participants in the morning service received an "Order of Service." This is not unusual, except that everything was timed to the minute (as if we were taping a radio or TV broadcast), including 14 minutes for the message—out of the 90 minute service.

Something is out of sync when the source of spiritual truth is viewed as ancillary to worship. Can we expect those who sit in the pew to hold a high view of Scripture when it is treated as incidental in the assembly of believers?

> **No believer will ever be any stronger spiritually that his knowledge and personal assimilation of God's Word into his head and heart. The more you know, understand, and obey the Word, the more Christ-like and less world-like you become.**

Ponder this. Why have many fellowships (denominations) ceased having Sunday evening services? The answer is usually something like, "We don't have enough people to pay the light bill." Pundits tell us that few people are willing to commit to church attendance for more than an hour to an hour and a half on Sunday morning. Even some evangelical and Pentecostal congregations are following this current trend.

Look below the surface.   Is the real reason for diminishing attendance the complexity of family or individual schedules? Would you agree that most of us do the things that are really important to us?   From personal recreational activities (this list would indeed be long) to watching a favorite TV program each day somehow we manage to *have, take,* or *make* the time to satisfy these desires.   I am not suggesting that one should abandon all forms relaxation or take on a monastic lifestyle. The point is far too many professing Christians see church attendance as a matter of choice—take it or leave it.   Some have even come to the conclusion that it is irrelevant to their lives.   Is it possible that one of the bottom line causes is spiritual malnutrition? Has their diet consisted of psychological motivation, self-esteem, and good works rather than the strong meat of the Word?

Not everyone will respond to a straight-forward presentation of the Word.   The prophets found this to be true.   John the Baptist experienced the same.   Even when our Lord pressed the claims of commitment to those who came searching for Him after the miracle of the loaves and fish, the Scriptures note, *"From this time many of his disciples turned back and no longer followed Him"* (John 6:66, NIV).   However, every record, both scriptural and historical, confirms that any genuine spiritual awakening was birthed by a specific and deliberate return to the Word of God.

• Equal time for the Word

In the Old Testament Book of Nehemiah is a moving record of the encounter the people who returned from Babylonian captivity had with God.   Let's look at several verses from the account.

"So on October 8 Ezra the priest brought the scroll of the law

before the assembly, which included men and women and all the children old enough to understand. (Notice who was in the congregation.) He faced the square just inside the Water Gate from early morning until noon and read aloud to everyone who could understand. All the people paid close attention to the Book of the Law. Ezra stood on the platform in full view of all the people. When they saw him open the book, they rose to their feet" (Nehemiah 8:1-3, 5, NLT, emphasis mine).

"They (Levites) read from the Book of the Law of God and clearly explained the meaning of what was being read, helping the people to understand each passage" (Nehemiah 8:8, NLT).

"On October 31 the people returned for another observance. This time they fasted and dressed in sackcloth and sprinkled dust on their heads. The Book of the Law of the Lord their God was read aloud to them for about three hours. Then for three more hours they took turns confessing their sins and worshipping the Lord their God" (Nehemiah 9:1, 3, NLT, emphasis mine).

Clearly the Word of God brought repentance and revival to that generation. It will be the same today.

• Will the real preacher please stand up

Preaching is decidedly a New Testament emphasis. There are more than <u>130 references</u> to the subject. Many of the named spiritual leaders of the Early Church are identified as preachers. As an aside, those who are in the preaching ministry have a distinctive call from God. No person should ever enter the ministry as a profession of personal choice. The Scriptures provide conclusive evidence that the hand of God specifically rests upon those whom He has chosen to represent Him as spokespersons. It is a sacred privilege to stand before any gathering of people and speak eternal truth on His behalf.

John the Baptist *"came preaching in the wilderness of Judea"* (Matthew 3:1).

Jesus *"went about all Galilee...preaching the gospel of the Kingdom"* (Matthew 4:3; 9:35, etc.).

The 12 Disciples *"went forth, and preached everywhere"* (Mark 16:20).

After the outpouring of the Holy Spirit at Pentecost, the **apostles** became powerful preachers of the Word. In fact, the Book of Acts alone records 36 references to preaching the gospel. After being beaten for preaching the gospel, "they ceased not to teach and preach Jesus Christ" (Acts 5:42).

Paul describes himself as being *"ordained a preacher, and an apostle"* and being *"appointed a preacher, and an apostle, and a teacher of the Gentiles"* in his two letters to Timothy (1 Timothy 2:7; 2 Timothy 1:11).

Among the 21 references to preaching in 1 and 2 Corinthians, Paul provides both the content and urgency of the message. *"Christ sent me not to baptize, but to preach the gospel"* (1 Corinthians 1:17). *"The preaching of the cross is to them that perish foolishness"* (1 Corinthians 1:18). *"We preach Christ crucified"* (I Corinthians 1:21). *"For though I preach the gospel, I have nothing to glory of: for necessity is laid upon me; yea, woe is me if I preach not the gospel"* (1 Corinthians 9:16).

Another pertinent aspect of this business of preaching relates to the preacher herself/himself. Only a few days into the life of the Early Church there was a dispute between the Hebrew and Greek widows. The apostles quickly dispelled any doubts about their main commitment. Speaking to the whole church body, they said, *"It would not be right for us to neglect the ministry of the Word of God in order to wait on tables...We will give our attention to prayer and the ministry of the Word"* (Acts 6:2-4, NIV). They recognized the high call of God to be His spokespersons.

Immediately someone counters that our culture is different. True. However, here the preacher must be diligent in leading the local congregation into a deep appreciation for the Word. While serving as senior pastor to a wonderful congregation, I pledged to them that I would not preach any sermon on Sunday morning that I had ever preached previously—anywhere. Consequently, I would spend 20 or more hours each week preparing that one sermon. (There were also the Sunday and Wednesday evening messages, along with a Sunday School lesson, and radio and TV broadcasts.) After some months, the congregation asked if we could begin the Sunday morning service earlier so there would be more time for the message. I preached almost one hour every Sunday morning. (Marcia says they ruined me for life.)

The bivocational pastor has time constraints that those who are provided adequate salaries do not have. God knows when we are doing the very best we can possibly do. I am convinced that He provides an anointing that could only come from the Spirit. However, **my plea is that every preacher of the gospel has such a passion for the Word that it will become contagious to the congregation**. Avoid the "Saturday night Special" (the term I give to those messages hurriedly taken from a sermon outline book late Saturday night) or the temptation to rely on the Spirit to give you a message as you begin to speak.

The study of the Word will excite your faith. Being able to say that the Spirit spoke this truth to my heart is powerful and spiritually uplifting to the believers in the pew.

Always be passionate about the gospel and preach with deep conviction. Preacher friend, be awake to the times. Don't be discouraged. Keep an open ear to the voice of the Spirit and turn a deaf ear to the nay sayers who are predicting gloom and despair for the Lord's Church. Preach the *whole counsel of God* faithfully. That is all the Master requires of any servant. God will honor His Word. It is His unfailing promise.

• Start where you are

1. <u>Know the biblical knowledge level of the congregation.</u>
   Remember that Jesus spoke differently to various audiences. To the multitudes, He frequently used parables and stories. The illustrations were commonly known and understood. Then, in private He explained the spiritual meaning of the message to the disciples. When Christ addressed the self-righteous religious leaders—those who were well versed in the Law of Moses—He spoke with a different emphasis. He had great compassion on the general population; He had little compassion for the teachers of the Law. Prepare your sermons so the hearers can comprehend how this translates into daily life. Applying Scripture appropriately is vitally important to most people in the pew. Remember, people are struggling just to make it through the next day. They need a word of assurance from the Lord.

2. <u>Preach doctrinal sermons frequently.</u>
   Before you decide that you do not like the word doctrine, I remind you that all the great themes of Scripture (inspiration of Scripture, deity of Christ, salvation by faith, heaven and hell, etc.) are doctrines. Paul had instructions for Timothy relating to this matter. In his two letters to his son in the faith, he refers to *doctrine* 13 times.

"If thou put the brethren in remembrance of these things, thou shalt be a good minister of Jesus Christ, nourished up in the words of faith and of a good doctrine, whereunto thou hast attained" (1 Timothy 4:6, emphasis mine).

"Till I come, give attendance to reading, to exhortation, and to doctrine" (1 Timothy 4:13, emphasis mine).

"Take heed unto thyself, and unto the doctrine; continue in them: for in doing this thou shalt both save thyself, and them that hear thee" (1 Timothy 4:16, emphasis mine).

"All scripture is given by inspiration of God, and is profitable for doctrine…" (1 Timothy 3:16, emphasis mine).

"Preach the Word; be instant in season, out of season; reprove, rebuke, exhort will all longsuffering and doctrine" (2 Timothy 4:2, emphasis mine).

Doctrinal preaching is scriptural preaching. It does not need to be boring or irrelevant to life. Great themes such as *justification by faith* or the *Resurrection* are often passed by under the assumption that everyone knows these truths. This kind of preaching is the diet young, immature believers need in order to grow. Watch their eyes light up as they understand how the Word is working within them. Their appetite for the Word will increase. Keep feeding them large portions of the Word. They will soon become strong, healthy disciples.

In today's culture, the preacher should never assume that the person in the pew knows even the simplest Bible stories. Since teaching of Scripture is forbidden in public education and often neglected at home, many in this generation have never heard of Daniel in the lion's den or Jonah in the belly of the whale. Be creative in your presentation, but don't forget the details. Your audience may not have a clue of what you are talking about or how to make a personal application of the truth.

Perhaps it would be helpful for the preacher to do a refresher course in Bible doctrine. Remember the textbook you used during your ministerial training. Pull the class notes out of the dusty file and allow the freshness of those truths to latch on to your spirit. Never become too sophisticated to preach John 3:16.

3. Use a variety of approaches in your preaching.

The presentation of a "series" can generate positive effects on the congregation. For example, in addition to providing new biblical information, such an extended series will often stimulate attendance or enhance the desire for personal study. Perhaps you may wish to consider one or more of the following ideas.

Biblical characters, such as Joseph or David are always relevant.

Books of the Bible, providing background information as to time written, why written, and the major theme(s). Often believers do not study simply because they do not understand the context in which God gave a particular message to His people.

Timely subjects, such as God's plan for the family or end-time events. Those topics that are close to where people live always generate an interest in how the Bible speaks to the issue.

I hesitate to include modern technology as a means of presenting the gospel lest some who do not have access to such would be discouraged. However, it must realistically be acknowledged that today's audience is savvy when it comes to computers and the concomitant methodologies readily available to almost every sector of society. Various approaches can be utilized. This is not an attempt to champion any particular pulpit style or the choice of visual enhancements to employ. We are in a life-death struggle for the eternal souls of men, and it is foolish to stubbornly stick our heels into the ground and not do everything possible to present Jesus Christ.

4. <u>Balance the preaching of the Word with appropriate expressions of worship.</u>

In short, provide an opportunity for people to respond to the preaching of the Word. The Holy Spirit will convince and convict; but, unless there is immediate action, the Spirit's voice will often fade in the routines of daily pressures. When the disciples went out to preach, the Scriptures note that there were verifiable results. The final verse in Mark's gospel (16:20) says it succinctly. *"Then the disciples went out and preached everywhere, and the Lord worked with them and confirmed His word by the signs that accompanied it."* Preaching an enlightening message and then immediately pronouncing the benediction only allows the Spirit to do a portion of His work. In earlier days we called it giving an altar invitation. Some are fearful to ask people to come forward lest they be offended and embarrassed.

On this count the words of Jesus come into sharp focus. *"If anyone is ashamed of me and my words in this adulterous and sinful generation, the Son of Man will be ashamed of him when he comes in the Father's glory with the holy angels"* (Mark 8:38, NIV).

There are times when the Word prompts a spontaneous response of praise, adoration, and worship. To stymie that is comparable to the second team that practices all week and then can only stand along the sidelines and watch. Pastor, preach for a response. Expect the Lord to speak to His people. Then open the door for the sweet breezes of heaven to flow over the earnest of heart.

While I have addressed some of the concerns facing the church today, it is encouraging to find among those who love the Lord supremely, that there is a longing to hear the uncompromised truth of the Book. Some of those dear saints find great delight in the Word and have never ceased interceding for revival and a return to holy living. *Anointed preaching is not an ancient relic suitable for the museum.* More than ever before in the history of mankind, the message of hope must go forth. Preacher, go into your study with determination and purpose. Fall on your face before God in spiritual preparation. Then, let the Word come alive in your heart so when you step in the pulpit it will not simply be one of the duties of the pastor; it will be the most exciting minutes of the entire week—for both you and the congregation.

Preach, brother and sister. PREACH!!

EMBRACING THE TRUTH

1. Preaching was a vital component in spreading the message of Christ during New Testament times. The apostles and Early Church leaders were deeply committed to preaching the Word of God. They prioritized their lives so other considerations were secondary to preaching.

2. The New Testament teaches that the **content** of the message is vital. Paul strongly urges the young pastor Timothy to carefully **guard the doctrine.**

3. **Revivals and spiritual awakenings** of both scripture and history were preceded by a **return to the Word of God.** The same is true in this generation.

4. Believers are no stronger spiritually than their **knowledge, understanding,** and **application** of the Word to their lives.

5. Those who are in the preaching ministry have a specific **call from God** upon their lives. Those who are so called have been granted a sacred privilege as spokespersons for the Almighty.

6. Contemporary culture offers strong competition to the church; however, the Word is God is powerful and will accomplish its eternal purpose.

7. Anointed, biblical preaching is urgently needed to call sinners to repentance and challenge lukewarm believers to a return to their first love.

CHAPTER TWELVE

THE COMING HEAD-ON COLLISION

"The weakness of the church is not that we are too uninvolved in the politics or administration of our society, but that we too easily absorb the false values of an unbelieving world. The problem is not too little activism, but too much assimilation."

John F. MacArthur, Jr.

The New Testament church flourished in an extremely hostile culture. As both political and religious assaults were mounting against this fledging group of spiritual firebrands, the more their numbers grew and the wider their sphere of influence spread. From the Day of Pentecost in Jerusalem to the revival in Samaria it was not long before the Jews stirred up the people of Thessalonica, saying, *"These that have turned the world upside down are come hither also"* (Acts 17:6). It was in Antioch, where Barnabas and Saul spent a full year discipling multitudes of both Jew and Greeks, that believers were *"first called Christians"* (Acts 11:26). The use of this title was by no means a term of endearment. In fact, the opposite was true. The WWJD (What Would Jesus Do) bracelets and necklaces would pale by comparison to their insistence that everything they did please Jesus Christ. They were so devout that identification as "Christian" was a moniker that the whole city immediately recognized.

Soon the Roman government became squeamish about this new sect. Their ambassadors were popping up everywhere. In his letter of thanks to the Philippian church for their generosity, Paul extends greetings from the other brothers in Rome and *"especially those who work in Caesar's palace"*

(Philippians 4:22, NLT). These Roman leaders turned up the pressure on the followers of Christ. Nero was especially hostile and violent. The first epistle of Peter deals with the theme of *"suffering"* (mentioned at least 15 times) as he encourages believers to be strong and faithful. In chapters 3 and 4, Peter instructs them not to be surprised if they face persecution. Rather, he encourages rejoicing in that suffering <u>for</u> Christ ultimately leads to eternal glory <u>with</u> Christ. Even though there was a bloodbath, including all the apostles except John, the church did not flinch. It grew stronger and stronger right in the middle of their antagonistic culture.

Vile, evil, immoral, amoral, hostile, self-serving, suave, philosophical, greedy, materialistic, or any descriptive adjective you add in front of the word culture, cannot *destroy*, *defeat*, or *damage* the true Church—unless the church itself allows it to happen. Historically, over an extended period cultural patterns slip into the church. One generation knew the reality of God's power and presence but their children and grandchildren were spectators and soon the significance of holy living began to fade away.

STEPS TO ACCEPTANCE OF AN UNACCEPTABLE PRINCIPLE OR PATTERN OF BEHAVIOR

1. Total rejection
2. Silent tolerance
3. Open consideration
4. Reluctant acceptance
5. Verbal propagation

I was the speaker for a Pentecost Sunday rally in which several churches of various doctrinal persuasions joined together. In the message, I mentioned that if one looked back only a few decades there would be an absolute rejection of certain things that are today being promoted by certain fellowships. When I said this, there was a cheer that went up from one section. After the service, I queried the host pastor. It seems that a group of about 150 had walked out of their Sunday morning service a few weeks earlier when the pastor had taken a stance in favor of ordaining homosexuals. The leaders of 50 years ago in that communion would turn over in their graves if they knew such was transpiring today.

• Disaster is imminent

The **true Church** is being *"built"* by the Lord just as He promised (Matthew 16:18) and even hell's gates will not prevent it from being accomplished according to the plan of God. The use of the word *"gates"* is significant. In the Old Testament the gates of a city symbolized its strength of fortification. (Samson embarrassed the Philistines by carrying off the gates of the city.) Jesus is telling His disciples that Satan's strongest defense—not offense—cannot stop the Church. Notice where He is building His Church. It is *"at the gate"* of Hell (Hades) itself, implying spiritual hand-to-hand combat.

As believers we are as close to hell as we ever need be. The Lord has positioned His church at this exact spot for a divine purpose. The church is the vanguard—the front line—to turn men and women away from rushing blindly into the place of eternal damnation.

The glorious, indisputable truth is that the plan of God will be fulfilled. So, dear saint of God, have no fear. His Word is as infallible today as it has ever been. Not one "i" will go undotted nor one "t" uncrossed until all has been completely and totally fulfilled. The frightening, indisputable truth is that it will be fulfilled *with or without us*.

1. Disaster is imminent—<u>when the authority of Scripture is questioned by those who profess to know Christ as Savior</u>. This is the inner rot of the spiritual tree. For a while it appears externally (attendance, finances, etc.) healthy. It is appalling to hear preachers and teachers of the Word spending hours trying to explain away the reality of God's message. This is not an attempt to point a finger or place blame. It is a plea for those who have been called to deliver the truth to do so with an unwavering personal confidence in the Book you present as *propositional truth*.

   <u>Professor</u>, in the name of scholarship do not leave your students confused and bewildered. They must not walk out of the classroom with uncertainty as to very basis of faith.

   <u>Pastor</u>, in the name of being relevant or intellectual or culturally acceptable, please do not depart from the simplicity of God's Word.

   Having been immeasurably blessed with a wide berth of ministerial experiences for more than four decades, I seldom stand in the pulpit today without making a direct reference to the authenticity and authority of the Scriptures. I want that audience to know that I wholeheartedly believe it and long for them to embrace its blessed truth.

2. Disaster is imminent—<u>when believers abandon a life of holiness and accept and adopt the unscriptural behavior of the unregenerate world</u>. "Fence-straddlers," we used to call them. Holding on to the hand of the Lord with one hand while holding on to the world with the other is not only a miserable way to live, it will soon lead to

spiritual defeat. Backsliders, at one time on fire for God now sit in the pew, sing the hymns and choruses, go through all the motions of serving the Lord, but are hiding sin in their lives. The breakdown of the scripturally ordained family structure—one man married to one woman for life—has left a trail of devastation that cannot be measured. Tragically, it is as common in the church as outside the church. Adultery is rampant.

Young people grow up assuming that fornication is no more sinful than holding hands. Men who serve as deacons, elders, Sunday School teachers, and in other leadership capacities dabbling with Internet pornography has reached epidemic proportions. Unwanted pregnancies terminated by abortion, often with parental approval. Youth groups attending vulgar movies or concerts as a church-sponsored activity. And, these are just the obvious. What about dishonest business dealings to make just one more dollar? Dare I mention honesty on tax returns or shading the truth for expediency?

A deacon told me, "Pastor, if you would just lighten up a bit, our church could really grow." Numbers are important—each represents a soul who needs Christ. But numbers for the sake of bragging rights is surely offensive to a holy God. At times, I confess to moments of deep introspection, wondering if this kind of message is shrugged off as coming from some other generation preacher. Friend, please hear my heart. Unless the church returns to its scriptural place of separation from this world, God's judgment is inevitable.

THE EXTERNAL EVIDENCE OF REVIVAL AMONG BELIEVERS IS A RETURN TO HOLY LIVING.

---

3. Disaster is imminent—<u>when the Church loses focus of its reason for existence in this world</u>. The sanctuary, with a seating capacity of 5,000, was constructed at the cost of $13 million. Debt retirement was almost overwhelming for the congregation. The facility is used now only for Sunday morning worship. All other meetings and activities are in the old sanctuary or other parts of the campus. Think about it—a $13 million structure in use for 2 hours per week!

The **Great Commission** (Matthew 28:18-20; Mark 16:15) is still the mandate for the church. So long as there is even one lost person on the face of the globe, the church cannot boast that it has completed its mission. However, there are two distinctive components in Christ's command to the disciples.

   a. *<u>Evangelism</u> of the lost is the initial step.</u>* Regardless of the cultural pressure for tolerance of all faiths and religions, there is still only one way for man to be saved. In the teachings of some religious leaders there can be found some good moral instruction. Some of the devotees to these religions often put Christians to shame by their commitment. However, these qualities do not erase the need for spiritually dead, depraved man to come to God through Jesus Christ. The message is: *"Salvation is found in <u>no one else</u>, for there is <u>no other name</u> under heaven given to men by which we <u>must be saved</u>"* (Acts 4:12, NIV, emphasis mine).

   b. *<u>Discipleship</u> of the converts* is vital to the building of the church. Often one hears astronomical numbers of converts in an evangelistic outreach. That is wonderful—provided that these newborn babes are nurtured and brought into the caring, loving atmosphere of a local church. Evangelism is not just so many notches in our belt. **The proof of evangelism is disciples. Spiritual maturity comes through systematic study of God's Word, the work of the Holy Spirit, diligent prayer, and fellowship with other believers.** It is a long process, requiring not only time but also patience. It will require a major investment of resources (both finances and leadership) in this process. Discipleship is a bit more than requiring attendance for three services a month in order to play on the church softball team. The biblical pattern was given by Paul to Timothy. *"And the things you have heard me say in the presence of many witnesses entrust to reliable men who will also be qualified to teach others"* (2 Timothy 2:2, NIV). By following these instructions, the church will grow geometrically rather than arithmetically.

**If the GREAT COMMISSION
is viewed as the**

**GREAT OPTION
it soon becomes the**

GREAT OMISSION

---

4. Disaster is imminent—<u>when the church becomes self-sufficient and independent</u>. Pride is a terrible thing, and we know God's attitude toward it. Peter says that *"God resists the proud"* (1 Peter 5:5). The word resist is a military term meaning to prepare for battle. Our pride often keeps us from admitting our pride. The church at Laodecia—the "lukewarm" crowd—had become self

sufficient in their attitude. Listen to the severity of the Lord's rebuke. *"You say, 'I am rich; I have acquired wealth and do not need a thing.' But you do not realize that you are wretched, pitiful, poor, blind and naked"* (Revelation 3:17, NIV). That is the foolishness of pride. They did not even realize how desperate the situation had become. Do we depend on schedules for a smooth-flowing service? Most evangelicals and Pentecostals reject the idea of a liturgy, but have we developed one of our own? Does the Spirit have free access into our worship or would He have to tear the Order of Service away from us to have a moment to speak? When can you last recall a time of intercessory prayer for revival?

One other observation should be made here. An attitude that shouts arrogantly, we have developed or discovered the methodology to grow a church, is extremely dangerous. Our patterns of worship are exciting; our methods of evangelism are cutting edge; our numbers are exploding; our finances are larger than at anytime in the history of this church. Yes sir, we are good and we know it. If God is blessing, remember it is His doing and not ours. Accept His favor with deep humility. Reflect on history. Some tried to assume God's glory unto themselves. God will not share His glory with anyone.

5. Disaster is imminent—when the Church loses sight of the soon return of Christ. *"This same Jesus...will come back in the same way you have seen Him go into heaven"* (Acts 1:11, NIV) was the angelic word to the disciples as they watched Christ disappear into the clouds. Those followers of Christ were motivated by this promise. Paul fully expected to be alive when the saints were raptured. In addressing the concerns of the believers in Thessalonica that Christ had not yet returned and some

of the believers had died, the apostle assures them they will be resurrected from the dead. Twice he says *"we who are still alive"* (1 Thessalonians 4: 15, 17), indicating his confidence that the coming of the Lord is near.

Peter, in his final letter, reminds the church that Christ is going to return. He will keep His promise, in spite of the *"scoffers"* who come in the *"last days"* making fun of the idea. Urging these followers of Christ to maintain a holy faith, Peter declares, "The day of the Lord will come like a thief" (2 Peter 3:10, NIV). The Book of Revelation concludes: *"He who testifies to these things says, 'Yes, I am coming soon.' Amen. Come, Lord Jesus. The grace of the Lord Jesus be with God's people. Amen"* (Revelation 22:20,21, NIV).

Songs bespeak of an era of time. Only old-timers will recall "When I've Gone the Last Mile of the Way" or "When I Take My Vacation in Heaven" or "We Shall See the King." Even the more recognized "I've Got A Mansion" hardly seems relevant to many today. This is not an appeal to return to that type song; rather, to illustrate that in earlier years the church was keenly anticipating the coming of the Lord.

And, that **Blessed Hope** produced numerous positive benefits in the New Testament church. <u>It stimulated evangelism.</u> If the Lord is coming soon, we must tell our family and friends to prepare to meet Him. <u>It encouraged holy living.</u> (I remember hoping that the Lord would not come because I had committed some terrible sin—at the age of 6 or 7.) John writes, *"Everyone who has this hope in him purifies himself, just as he is pure"* (1 John 3:3, NIV). <u>It generated loving unity.</u> If the "Sweet By and By" was just one street over, then it is imperative that we learn to live in peaceful harmony now. No wonder this joyous group loved to be together. It was a little foretaste of heaven.

Preacher, when have you painted a picture of heaven that was so real that the people in the pew thought you were planning a trip that day? What about a sermon that depicted the coming judgment of God upon this world? You say, " Ah, yes, but my folks are not into that kind of thing. It's surreal. That pie-in-the-sky sort of thing offends them. You know, it is an affront to their intelligence." Dear brother, it is God's Word. Jesus is coming soon. Begin to declare this truth with the same passion that you preach salvation. It may surprise you to see how many lives are impacted for righteousness.

- ## It's decision time

The church stands at a major crossroad. A decision with incalculable consequence looms before us. How we respond will dramatically impact the future. Those of us who have lived through a significant period of history have witnessed the ebb and flow of spiritual tides in the church. However, the church has allowed the disconcerting cultural events of the past half century to fling it into a downward spiral of frightening magnitude.

1. The sexual revolution which began in the 1960s has continued to escalate until today there are few, if any, cultural restraints. From the free love of the hippie generation to the granting of equal status to homosexual and lesbian couples, moral virtues viewed as sacred by an earlier society have been drowned in a cesspool of filth and vulgarity. One who dares to speak against such immorality is characterized as a puritanical prude.

2. <u>The assault on the family/home</u>, especially coming into the home through the media, has been relentless. TV sitcoms picture parents as imbecilic. Adultery and fornication are the norm for many programs. The subsequent rate of divorce, the dysfunctional families and children with several sets of parents is almost incomprehensible. The anger that has developed from not following scriptural principles in the home has found expression in mass murders in the classroom, vandalism for no reason, and a sullen, rebellious attitude toward parental authority. Drug and alcohol use have found the vulnerable on the elementary school campus. With such poor earthly examples of a loving Heavenly Father, the church has been hard put to convince this generation there really is a God who cares about them.

3. <u>The developing mistrust of political leaders</u>, from Watergate to the next scandal, in the Congress, in the state house, or in local government has fostered a skeptical attitude toward authority. It has reared its head in church after church until many pastors walk off disillusioned and broken. Honesty demands that we add to all of this the glaring sins of highly visible leaders in the church. Believers should keep their eyes on the Lord and not look at the failure of men. But try convincing tender, young believers who has been marginalized or rejected by society and now find that their spiritual hero behaves no differently from the double standard they have observed at home, on the job, or in the political arena. It can be devastating.

The shifts in the cultural landscape have been dramatic—from a relatively unified moral standard to a horrid unleashing of demonic forces. *If there is blame to be placed for what has devolved in the church, an accusing finger cannot be pointed at society in general. The responsibility must be shouldered by the church itself.* To the degree that our culture has deterred us from scriptural principles and practice, it is our fault. If we could not have lived above the world, our Lord would have told us. What He did tell us was exactly the opposite. We are guilty. No excuses. No rationalization.

Is it too late? No! God is longsuffering. The record of Scripture testifies that He will forgive and restore. But there are some things that we (individually and collectively) must do immediately.

1. REPENT
Plead with God for mercy. Ask His forgiveness for known sin. Ask him to show you any area of failure that you are unaware of. Intercede for your local church. Believe that He will hear your broken heart and bring healing and restoration to fellow believers. Pray for your pastor and the spiritual leaders in your fellowship that they will experience a fresh empowering of the Holy Spirit for ministry.

2. ABANDON SIN
Search the Scriptures diligently. Ask the Holy Spirit to reveal the principles of holiness and righteous to you. Leave those things that defeat and destroy your spiritual life. If you have a question about a specific thing—is it or is it not wrong—forsake it. Be willing to lay aside even those legitimate areas of life for Christ's sake.

3. GIVE PRIORITY TO THE MISSION/MINISTRY OF THE CHURCH
View daily life and its concomitant responsibilities in

the light of eternal values. Develop a worldview of the mission of the church. See the urgency of sharing the gospel in your own community and all around the globe. Make yourself available for service in any and every way possible. Allow the Holy Spirit to develop and mature you as a spiritual leader in the local fellowship of believers with whom you worship.

4. **BE PASSIONATE ABOUT YOUR FAITH**
This is life or death—heaven or hell. Do not be intimidated by the agnostics, skeptics, or even less committed believers. Share you faith, both in word and by your lifestyle. Never be hesitant to testify of God's grace and goodness in your own life. Invite others to accept Christ. Ask them to attend church with you.

5. **LEAD YOUR HOME/FAMILY INTO GODLINESS**
Follow scriptural principles for husband-wife relationships. Bring up your children to love God and respect His house. Monitor carefully the things that you allow into your home (TV programs, videos, music). Guard your time together so that home is truly a sanctuary from the powerful sinful influences encountered each day in the world.

6. **LIVE EACH DAY IN HOPE OF HIS RETURN**
Rise every morning with the hope that this could be the day of our blessed Lord's return to earth. Retire each night with a prayer of anticipation that He will come before the sun rises in the morning. Face the difficulties of life by His abundant grace, knowing that life is brief, the trials are for our benefit, preparing us for that glorious eternal day.

7. BE WILLING TO FACE PERSECUTION

Tomorrow our culture may move further away from God. It could well mean that believers will feel the hand of Satan as he uses his emissaries in an attempt to eradicate the church of Jesus Christ from the earth. Remember, our suffering for Him is rewarded greatly by our glory with Him.

FINALLY, BRETHREN...

You have heard my heart. I have made myself vulnerable in sharing the deep burden I feel. I love the Church. It has been the center of my universe from my earliest childhood. It has been a long journey from a Junior Boys Sunday School class where I first heard the call of God to preach the gospel. Someday I want to hear Him say, *"Well done."*

Many of you, colleagues in ministry, have wept and cried over the present state of the church. Please don't stop now. Perhaps this will be the moment of divine intervention for your flock.

Over the years, in hundreds of churches, I have met thousands of choice saints who have spent hours in the closet of prayer seeking God for revival and the church to be restored to its rightful place of heavenly glory. Hold on, dear, faithful intercessor. The answer is on the way.

"Christ loved the church, and gave Himself for it; that He might sanctify and cleanse it with the washing of water by the word, that He might present it to himself a glorious church, not having spot, or wrinkle, or any such thing; but that it should be holy and without blemish" (Ephesians 5:25,26).

ADDITIONAL BOOKS
by

H. Maurice Lednicky

The Scriptures Applied, Volume I

The Scriptures Applied, Volume II

The Scriptures Applied, Volume III

Insights from the Word: A Collection of Scriptural Truth

ORDER FROM

LIFESTYLE MINISTRIES
1431 East Burntwood
Springfield, Missouri 65803
417-833-0349

mmlednicky@aol.com